Let's Get Cooking

MUG
CAKES

Over **100** indulgent recipes

igloobooks

Published in 2017
by Igloo Books Ltd
Cottage Farm
Sywell
NN6 0BJ
www.igloobooks.com

Designed by Nicholas Gage
Edited by Jasmin Peppiatt

Cover image: © iStock / Getty Images

LEO002 0717
2 4 6 8 10 9 7 5 3 1
ISBN 978-1-78670-606-5

Printed and manufactured in China

Contents

Classic

MAKES: 2 | PREP TIME: **30 MINS** | COOKING TIME: **1 MIN 30 SECS**

Vanilla Mug Cake

55 g / 2 oz / ¼ cup butter, softened

55 g / 2 oz / ¼ cup caster
(superfine) sugar

1 large egg

½ tsp vanilla extract

55 g / 2 oz / ⅓ cup self-raising flour, sifted

TO DECORATE

30 g / 1 oz / ½ cup butter, softened

75 g / 2 ½ oz / ¾ cup icing
(confectioner's) sugar, plus extra
for dusting

½ tsp vanilla extract

½ vanilla pod, split lengthways

1. Beat the butter and sugar together in a mug until pale and smooth.
2. Break the egg into a second mug and add the vanilla extract. Beat gently with a fork, then gradually stir the egg into the butter mixture.
3. Fold in the flour and then spoon half of the mixture into the mug you used to beat the egg and level the tops.
4. Transfer the mugs to a microwave and cook on full power for 1 ½ minutes. Test the cakes by inserting a skewer into the centre – if it comes out clean, the cakes are ready. If not, return to the microwave for 15 seconds and test again.
5. Leave the cakes to cool completely.
6. Beat the butter, icing sugar and vanilla extract together until pale and well whipped, adding a few drops of hot water if the mixture is too stiff.
7. Spoon the buttercream into a piping bag fitted with a large star nozzle and pipe a big swirl on top of each cake.
8. Scrape the seeds out of the vanilla pod and dot them on top of the buttercream.

Chocolate Mug Cake

40 g / 1 ½ oz / ¼ cup self-raising flour
40 g / 1 ½ oz / ¼ cup caster
  (superfine) sugar
20 g cocoa powder
1 medium egg
2 tbsp milk
2 tbsp vegetable oil
1 tbsp chocolate chips
1 tsp icing (confectioner's) sugar

1. Mix the flour, sugar and cocoa in a large mug.
2. Add the egg and thoroughly mix.
3. Combine the milk and oil in another mug and add to the batter and stir.
4. Fold in the chocolate chips.
5. Place the mug in the centre of the microwave and cook for 1 ½ minutes on full power.
6. Check the cake by placing a skewer into the centre of the cake; it should come out clean when fully cooked.
7. Sprinkle with icing sugar and serve.

Simple Mug Cakes

55 g / 2 oz / ¼ cup butter, softened
55 g / 2 oz / ¼ cup caster (superfine) sugar
1 large egg
55 g / 2 oz / ⅓ cup self-raising flour, sifted

1. Beat the butter and sugar together in a mug until pale and smooth.
2. Break the egg into a second mug and beat it gently with a fork, then gradually stir the egg into the butter mixture.
3. Fold in the flour, then spoon half of the mixture into the mug you used to beat the egg and level the tops.
4. Transfer the mugs to a microwave and cook on full power for 1 minute 30 seconds. Test the cakes by inserting a skewer into the centre – if it comes out clean, they are ready. If not, return to the microwave for 15 seconds and test again.
5. Leave the cakes to cool for 5 minutes.
6. Serve on their own or with a flavoursome topping (see Toppings chapter).

MAKES: **1** | PREP TIME: **5 MINS** | COOKING TIME: **1 MIN 30 SECS**

Victoria Sponge Mug Cake

30 g / 1 oz / ⅛ cup butter
30 g / 1 oz / ⅛ cup caster (superfine) sugar
1 medium egg
30 g / 1 oz / ⅛ cup self-raising flour
1 tbsp milk
1 tsp vanilla extract
1 tbsp strawberry jam (jelly), sieved

TO DECORATE
1 tsp caster (superfine) sugar
fresh strawberries

1. Mix the butter and sugar in a large mug.
2. Add the egg and stir until well mixed.
3. Gradually stir in the flour and add the milk and vanilla extract; mix well.
4. Drop in the strawberry jam and allow to sink into the mixture without stirring.
5. Place the mug in the centre of the microwave and cook for 1 ½ minutes until well risen or until a skewer inserted in the centre comes out clean.
6. Sprinkle caster sugar on top and garnish with fresh strawberries.

MAKES: 2 | PREP TIME: 30 MINS | COOKING TIME: 16 MINS

Date and Walnut Mug Cake

55 g / 2 oz / ¼ cup butter, softened
55 g / 2 oz / ¼ cup caster
  (superfine) sugar
1 large egg
55 g / 2 oz / ⅓ cup self-raising flour, sifted
¼ tsp ground cinnamon
2 tsp walnuts, finely chopped
2–3 large dates, stoned and
  finely chopped

TO DECORATE
30 g / 1 oz / ½ cup butter, softened
75 g / 2 ½ oz / ¾ cup icing
  (confectioner's) sugar, plus extra
  for dusting
½ tsp vanilla extract
2 large dates, stoned
4 walnut halves

1. Preheat the oven to 160°C (140°C fan) / 350F / gas 4.
2. Beat the butter and sugar together in an ovenproof mug until pale and smooth.
3. Break the egg into a second ovenproof mug. Beat gently with a fork, then gradually stir the egg into the butter mixture.
4. Fold in the flour, ground cinnamon, chopped walnuts and dates, then spoon half of the mixture into the mug you used to beat the egg and level the tops.
5. Transfer the mugs to a baking tray and cook in the centre of the oven for 16 minutes. Test the cakes by inserting a skewer into the centre – if it comes out clean, they're ready. If not, return to the oven for a couple of minutes and test again. Leave the cakes to cool completely.
6. Beat the butter, icing sugar and vanilla extract together until pale and smooth adding a few drops of hot water if the mixture is too stiff.
7. Spoon the buttercream into a piping bag fitted with a large plain nozzle and pipe a pillow on top of each cake. Top with a date and two walnut halves, then dust with icing sugar to serve.

Ginger Mug Cake

30 g / 1 oz / ⅛ cup butter, softened
30 g / 1 oz / ⅛ cup caster (superfine) sugar
1 medium egg
30 g / 1 oz / ⅛ cup self-raising flour
½ tsp ground ginger
1 tbsp milk
1 tbsp ginger conserve

TO DECORATE
1 tbsp ginger conserve or candied
   ginger pieces

1. Mix the butter and sugar in a large mug.
2. Add the egg and stir until well mixed.
3. Gradually stir in the flour and ginger.
4. Add the milk and mix well.
5. Fold in the ginger conserve.
6. Place the mug in the centre of the microwave and cook for 1 ½ minutes until well
    risen or until a skewer inserted in the centre comes out clean.
7. Top with more ginger conserve or candied ginger to serve.

Lemon Drizzle Mug Cake

30 g / 1 oz / ⅛ cup butter
30 g / 1 oz / ⅛ cup caster (superfine) sugar
1 medium egg
30 g / 1 oz / ⅛ cup self-raising flour
1 tbsp milk
lemon slice to decorate

FOR THE SYRUP
1 tbsp caster (superfine) sugar
1 tbsp boiling water
zest and juice of half a lemon

1. Preheat the oven to 180°C (160°C fan) / 425F / gas 4.
2. In a mug, combine 1 tbsp caster sugar with 1 tbsp boiling water. Stir in half of the
    lemon juice and cook in the centre of the microwave for 30 seconds. Allow to cool.
3. In a clean mug, mix the butter and sugar. Add the egg and stir until well mixed.
4. Gradually stir in the flour, then add the milk and mix well. Stir in the zest and
    remaining lemon juice.
5. Place the mug in the centre of the oven and cook for 10-12 minutes until well risen
    or until a skewer inserted in the centre comes out clean. Pour the lemon syrup over
    the cake whilst it is still warm.
6. Decorate with a lemon slice and serve.

MAKES: 1 | PREP TIME: 5 MINS | COOKING TIME: 1 MIN 30 SECS

Coconut Mug Cake

30 g / 1 oz / ⅛ cup butter
30 g / 1 oz / ⅛ cup caster (superfine) sugar
1 medium egg
30 g / 1 oz / ⅛ cup self-raising flour
1 tbsp milk
1 tbsp desiccated coconut

TO SERVE
1 scoop of coconut ice cream
1 tsp desiccated coconut

1. Mix the butter and sugar in a large mug.
2. Add the egg and stir until well mixed.
3. Gradually stir in the flour, then add the milk and mix well.
4. Fold in the coconut.
5. Place the mug in the centre of the microwave and cook for 1 ½ minutes until well risen or until a skewer inserted in the centre comes out clean.
6. Top with coconut ice cream, sprinkle with a little desiccated coconut and serve immediately.

MAKES: 2 | **PREP TIME: 30 MINS** | **COOKING TIME: 1 MIN 30 SECS**

Coffee and Walnut Mug Cake

55 g / 2 oz / ¼ cup butter, softened

55 g / 2 oz / ¼ cup caster (superfine) sugar

1 large egg

55 g / 2 oz / ⅓ cup self-raising flour, sifted

1 tsp instant espresso powder or 1 tsp coffee essence

1 tbsp cocoa powder

1 tbsp walnuts, finely chopped

TO DECORATE

30 g / 1 oz / ½ cup butter, softened

75 g / 2 ½ oz / ¾ cup icing (confectioner's) sugar

½ tsp instant espresso powder or 1 tsp coffee essence

1 tbsp walnuts, finely chopped

4 chocolate coffee beans

1. Beat the butter and sugar together in a mug until pale and smooth.

2. Break the egg into a second mug and beat gently with a fork, then gradually stir the egg into the butter mixture.

3. Fold in the flour, espresso powder / coffee essence and cocoa powder. Stir through the chopped walnut pieces. Spoon half of the mixture into the mug you used to beat the egg and level the tops.

4. Transfer the mugs to a microwave and cook on full power for 1 ½ minutes. Test the cakes by inserting a skewer into the centre – if it comes out clean, they're ready. If not, return to the microwave for 15 seconds and test again. Leave the cakes to cool completely.

5. Beat the butter, icing sugar and espresso powder / coffee essence together until pale and well whipped, adding a few drops of hot water if the mixture is too stiff.

6. Use a piping bag with a large star nozzle to pipe buttercream onto the cakes in a large swirl, decorate with chopped walnuts and chocolate coffee beans.

Cherry Mug Cake

30 g / 1 oz / ⅛ cup butter
30 g / 1 oz / ⅛ cup caster (superfine) sugar
1 medium egg
30 g / 1 oz / ⅛ cup self-raising flour
1 tbsp milk
2 tbsp glacé cherries, halved

1. Mix the butter and sugar in a large mug.
2. Add the egg and stir until well mixed.
3. Gradually stir in the flour, then add the milk and mix well.
4. Fold in the cherries.
5. Place the mug in the centre of the microwave and cook for 1 ½ minutes until well risen or until a skewer inserted in the centre comes out clean.

Raspberry and Vanilla Mug Cakes

55 g / 2 oz / ¼ cup butter, softened
55 g / 2 oz / ¼ cup caster (superfine) sugar
1 large egg
55 g / 2 oz / ⅓ cup self-raising flour, sifted
6 fresh raspberries

TO DECORATE

30 g / 1 oz / ½ cup butter, softened
75 g / 2 ½ oz / ¾ cup icing (confectioner's) sugar, plus extra for dusting
½ tsp vanilla extract
2 fresh raspberries

1. Beat the butter and sugar together in a mug until pale and smooth.
2. Break the egg into a second mug. Beat gently with a fork, then gradually stir the egg into the butter mixture.
3. Fold in the flour, then spoon half of the mixture into the mug you used to beat the egg. Push three raspberries down into the centre of each one and level the tops.
4. Transfer the mugs to a microwave and cook on full power for 1 minute 30 seconds. Test the cakes by inserting a skewer into the centre – if it comes out clean, they are ready. If not, return to the microwave for 15 seconds and test again. Leave the cakes to cool completely.
5. Beat the butter, icing sugar and vanilla extract together until pale and well whipped, adding a few drops of hot water if the mixture is too stiff.
6. Spoon the buttercream into a piping bag fitted with a large star nozzle and pipe a big swirl on top of each cake. Top each one with a raspberry.

MAKES: **2** | PREP TIME: **15 MINS** | COOKING TIME: **4 MINS**

Carrot Mug Cake

60 g / 2 oz / ¼ cup self-raising flour
30 g / 1 oz / ⅛ cup brown sugar
a pinch of salt
¼ tsp ground cinnamon, plus extra for sprinkling
2 tbsp vegetable oil
1 medium egg
1 tbsp milk
30 g / 1 oz / ⅛ cup carrot, finely grated

FOR THE FROSTING
30 g / 1 oz / ⅛ cup cream cheese
30 g / 1 oz / ⅛ cup icing (confectioner's) sugar

1. Mix the dry ingredients in a bowl.
2. Mix the wet ingredients in another bowl and add the carrot and stir until well mixed.
3. Combine the two mixtures and divide between two mugs.
4. Place one of the mugs in the centre of the microwave and cook for 2 minutes.
   Check the cake after 1 ½ minutes by placing a skewer in the centre of the mug.
   If the skewer comes out clean, the cake is ready. Repeat with the second mug.
   Allow to cool.
5. To make the frosting, mix the cream cheese with the icing sugar.
6. Top the cooled carrot cakes with the frosting and dust with a little cinnamon
   before serving.

MAKES: **2** | PREP TIME: **20 MINS** | COOKING TIME: **1 MIN 30 SECS**

Lemon Curd Mug Cake

55 g / 2 oz / ¼ cup butter, softened
55 g / 2 oz / ¼ cup caster
  (superfine) sugar
1 lemon, zest finely grated
1 large egg
55 g / 2 oz / ⅓ cup self-raising flour, sifted
2 tbsp lemon curd

TO DECORATE
1 tsp lemon juice
55 g / 2 oz / ½ cup icing
  (confectioner's) sugar

1. Beat the butter, sugar and lemon zest together in a mug until pale and smooth.

2. Break the egg into a second mug and beat gently with a fork, then gradually stir the egg into the butter mixture.

3. Fold in the flour, followed by the lemon curd, and then spoon half of the mixture into the mug you used to beat the egg.

4. Transfer the mugs to a microwave and cook on full power for 1 ½ minutes. Test the cakes by inserting a skewer into the centre – if it comes out clean, the cakes are ready. If not, return to the microwave for 15 seconds and test again.

5. Leave the cakes to cool for at least 10 minutes while you make the icing. Stir the lemon juice into the icing sugar a few drops at a time until thick but pourable. Drizzle the icing over the cakes and serve warm or at room temperature.

MAKES: **2** | PREP TIME: **30 MINS** | COOKING TIME: **1 MIN 30 SECS**

Marzipan Mug Cake

55 g / 2 oz / ¼ cup butter, softened

55 g / 2 oz / ¼ cup caster
(superfine) sugar

1 large egg

½ tsp almond extract

55 g / 2 oz / ⅓ cup self-raising flour, sifted

1 tbsp marzipan, cut into small chunks

TO DECORATE

1 small block of marzipan

icing (confectioner's) sugar for dusting

1. Beat the butter and sugar together in a mug until pale and smooth.
2. Break the egg into a second mug and add the almond extract. Beat gently with a fork, then gradually stir the egg into the butter mixture.
3. Fold in the flour and marzipan chunks then spoon half of the mixture into the mug you used to beat the egg and level the tops.
4. Transfer the mugs to a microwave and cook on full power for 1 ½ minutes. Test the cakes by inserting a skewer into the centre – if it comes out clean, they're ready. If not, return to the microwave for 15 seconds and test again. Leave the cakes to cool completely.
5. Roll out the marzipan on a lightly dusted surface until it is approximately ½ cm (¼ in) thick, then cut out two circles to match the size of the mug tops. Top each cake with a marzipan circle.
6. Roll the remaining marzipan into balls and toast for a few seconds with a kitchen blow torch until lightly browned. Arrange the balls around the mug tops.
7. Dust with icing sugar and serve.

MAKES: **2** | PREP TIME: **20 MINS** | COOKING TIME: **1 MIN 30 SECS**

Cinnamon and Raisin Mug Cake

55 g / 2 oz / ¼ cup butter, softened
55 g / 2 oz / ¼ cup caster (superfine) sugar
1 large egg
55 g / 2 oz / ⅓ cup self-raising flour, sifted
1 tsp ground cinnamon
1 tbsp raisins
1 tbsp cinnamon sugar
1 cinnamon stick, halved

1. Beat the butter and sugar together in a mug until pale and smooth.
2. Break the egg into a second mug and beat gently with a fork, then gradually stir the egg into the butter mixture.
3. Fold in the flour and ground cinnamon, followed by the raisins, then spoon half of the mixture into the mug used to beat the egg and level the tops.
4. Transfer the mugs to a microwave and cook on full power for 1 ½ minutes. Test the cakes by inserting a skewer into the centre – if it comes out clean, they're ready. If not, return to the microwave for 15 seconds and test again.
5. Sprinkle the top of the cakes with cinnamon sugar and brown them lightly under a hot grill. Serve warm or at room temperature, garnished with cinnamon stick halves.

MAKES: **2** | PREP TIME: **30 MINS** | COOKING TIME: **1 MIN 30 SECS**

Honey and Lemon Mug Cake

55 g / 2 oz / ¼ cup butter, softened

55 g / 2 oz / ¼ cup caster
(superfine) sugar

1 large egg

2 tbsp runny honey

2 tbsp lemon juice

55 g / 2 oz / ⅓ cup self-raising flour, sifted

½ unwaxed lemon, zested

TO DECORATE

30 g / 1 oz / ½ cup butter, softened

75 g / 2 ½ oz / ¾ cup icing
(confectioner's) sugar

2 tbsp runny honey plus a little extra
for drizzling

½ tsp lemon extract

2 thick slices of unwaxed lemon

1. Beat the butter and sugar together in a mug until pale and silky.

2. Break the egg into a second mug and add the runny honey and lemon juice. Beat gently with a fork, then gradually stir the egg into the butter mixture.

3. Fold in the flour and lemon zest and then spoon half of the mixture into the mug you used to beat the egg and level the tops.

4. Transfer the mugs to a microwave and cook on full power for 1 ½ minutes. Test the cakes by inserting a skewer into the centre – if it comes out clean, they're ready. If not, return to the microwave for 20 seconds and test again. Leave the cakes to cool completely.

5. Beat the butter, icing sugar, honey and lemon extract together until pale and well whipped, adding a few drops of hot water if the mixture is too stiff.

6. Spread the buttercream evenly on top of the cakes with a palette knife.

7. Top each cake with a slice of lemon drizzled with a little honey and serve.

Banana Mug Cake

55 g / 2 oz / ¼ cup butter, softened
55 g / 2 oz / ¼ cup caster (superfine) sugar
1 large egg
½ tsp vanilla extract
55 g / 2 oz / ⅓ cup self-raising flour, sifted
1 large banana, lightly mashed
6–8 dried banana chips

TO DECORATE
icing (confectioner's) sugar for dusting

1. Preheat the oven to 160°C (140°C fan) / 350F / gas 4.
2. Beat the butter and sugar together in an ovenproof mug until pale and smooth.
3. Break the egg into a second ovenproof mug and add the vanilla extract.
   Beat gently with a fork, then gradually stir the egg into the butter mixture.
4. Fold in the flour and the mashed banana, then spoon half of the mixture into the mug you used to beat the egg and level the tops.
5. Top the cakes with banana chips, laying them flat onto the surface of the mixture.
6. Transfer the mugs to a baking tray and cook in the centre of the oven for 16 minutes. Test the cakes by inserting a skewer into the centre – if it comes out clean, they're ready. If not, return to the oven for a couple of minutes and test again. Leave the cakes to cool a little and firm up.
7. Dust with icing sugar and serve warm with fresh cream.

Egg-free Strawberry Mug Cakes

55 g / 2 oz / ¼ cup butter, softened
55 g / 2 oz / ¼ cup caster (superfine) sugar
2 tbsp Greek yogurt
1 tsp orange zest, finely grated
55 g / 2 oz / ⅓ cup self-raising flour, sifted
4 strawberries, halved

1. Beat the butter and sugar together in a mug until pale and smooth, then beat in the yogurt and orange zest.
2. Fold in the flour, then spoon half of the mixture into a second mug. Push two strawberry halves down into each one and level the tops.
3. Transfer the mugs to a microwave and cook on full power for 1 minute 30 seconds. Test the cakes by inserting a skewer into the centre – if it comes out clean, they're ready. If not, return to the microwave for 15 seconds and test again.
4. Leave the cakes to cool for 5 minutes before serving, topped with the rest of the strawberries.

MAKES: 2 | **PREP TIME: 30 MINS** | **COOKING TIME: 1 MIN 30 SECS**

Maple and Pecan Mug Cake

55 g / 2 oz / ¼ cup butter, softened
55 g / 2 oz / ¼ cup caster
   (superfine) sugar
1 large egg
2 tsp natural maple syrup
55 g / 2 oz / ⅓ cup self-raising
   flour, sifted
8 pecan nuts, finely chopped

TO DECORATE
30 g / 1 oz / ½ cup butter, softened
75 g / 2 ½ oz / ¾ cup icing
   (confectioner's) sugar, plus extra
   for dusting
2 tsp natural maple syrup
10 pecan nuts, finely chopped

1. Beat the butter and sugar together in a mug until pale and smooth.
2. Break the egg into a second mug and add the maple syrup. Beat gently with a fork, then gradually stir the egg into the butter mixture.
3. Fold in the flour and chopped pecan nuts, then spoon half of the mixture into the mug you used to beat the egg and level the tops.
4. Transfer the mugs to a microwave and cook on full power for 1 ½ minutes. Test the cakes by inserting a skewer into the centre – if it comes out clean, they're ready. If not, return to the microwave for 15 seconds and test again. Leave the cakes to cool completely.
5. Beat the butter, icing sugar and 1 teaspoon of maple syrup together until pale and well whipped, adding a few drops of hot water if the mixture is too stiff.
6. Spread the buttercream onto each cake and level with a palette knife. Dot a few drops of maple syrup around the edge of the buttercream.
7. Arrange the pecan nut quarters in a flower in the centre of each cake and dust with a little icing sugar.

White Chocolate Mug Cake

55 g / 2 oz / ¼ cup butter, softened
55 g / 2 oz / ¼ cup caster (superfine) sugar
1 large egg
55 g / 2 oz / ⅓ cup self-raising flour, sifted
1 tbsp white chocolate chunks

TO DECORATE
100 g / 3 ½ oz / ⅔ bar of white chocolate
2 white chocolate cigarillos
2 plain chocolate cigarillos

1. Beat the butter and sugar together in a mug until pale and smooth.
2. Break the egg into a second mug. Beat gently with a fork, then gradually stir the egg into the butter mixture. Fold in the flour followed by the white chocolate chunks, then spoon half of the mixture into the mug you used to beat the egg and level the tops.
3. Transfer the mugs to a microwave and cook on full power for 1 ½ minutes. Test the cakes by inserting a skewer into the centre – if it comes out clean, they're ready. If not, return to the microwave for 15 seconds and test again. Leave the cakes to cool completely.
4. Melt the white chocolate over a bain-marie, saving a couple of pieces for making shavings. Spread each cake with melted chocolate and allow to cool a little. As the chocolate begins to harden, stick a white and a dark chocolate cigarillo into each cake. After the melted chocolate has set, make some chocolate shavings with the reserved white chocolate by shaving with a sharp paring knife.
5. Sprinkle the top of each cake with the chocolate shavings.

Vegan Pumpkin Mug Cakes

50 ml / 1 ¾ oz / ¼ cup maple syrup
50 ml / 1 ¾ oz / ¼ cup soya milk
2 tbsp sunflower oil
50 ml / 1 ¾ fl. oz / ¼ cup canned pumpkin puree
75 g / 2 ½ oz / ½ cup self-raising flour, sifted
½ tsp pumpkin pie spice mix, plus extra for sprinkling

1. Beat the maple syrup, milk, oil and pumpkin puree together in a large mug until pale and smooth.
2. Fold in the flour and pumpkin pie spice, then divide the mixture between four greased espresso cups and level the tops.
3. Transfer the cups to a microwave and cook on full power for 45 seconds. Test the cakes by inserting a skewer into the centre – if it comes out clean, they're ready. If not, return to the microwave for 10 seconds and test again.
4. Sprinkle with a little extra pie spice and serve warm or at room temperature.

MAKES: 1 | PREP TIME: 5 MINS | COOKING TIME: 1 MIN 30 SECS

Chocolate Chip Mug Cake

30 g / 1 oz / ⅛ cup butter, softened

30 g / 1 oz / ⅛ cup caster (superfine) sugar

1 medium egg

30 g / 1 oz / ⅛ cup self-raising flour

1 tbsp milk

1 tbsp large chocolate chips

2 tsp orange marmalade

1. Mix the butter and sugar in a large mug.
2. Add the egg and stir until well mixed.
3. Gradually stir in the flour, then add the milk and mix well.
4. Fold in the chocolate chips and marmalade, reserving a little of each for the top.
5. Place the mug in the centre of the microwave and cook for 1 ½ minutes until well risen or until a skewer inserted in the centre comes out clean. Allow to cool, then drizzle a little marmalade and sprinkle the chocolate chips onto the top.

MAKES: **2** | PREP TIME: **15 MINS** | COOKING TIME: **1 MIN 30 SECS**

Confetti Mug Cakes

55 g / 2 oz / ¼ cup butter, softened
55 g / 2 oz / ¼ cup light muscovado sugar
1 large egg
½ tsp vanilla extract
55 g / 2 oz / ⅓ cup self-raising flour, sifted
1 tbsp heart-shaped sugar confetti

1. Beat the butter and sugar together in a mug until pale and smooth.
2. Break the egg into a second mug and add the vanilla extract. Beat gently with a fork, then gradually stir the egg into the butter mixture.
3. Fold in the flour, then spoon half of the mixture into the mug you used to beat the egg and level the tops.
4. Transfer the mugs to a microwave and cook on full power for 1 minute 30 seconds. Test the cakes by inserting a skewer into the centre – if it comes out clean, they are ready. If not, return to the microwave for 15 seconds and test again.
5. Leave the cakes to cool for 5 minutes before serving, sprinkled with sugar confetti.

MAKES: 2 | PREP TIME: 30 MINS | COOKING TIME: 1 MIN 30 SECS

Chocolate Hazelnut Mug Cake

55 g / 2 oz / ¼ cup butter, softened

55 g / 2 oz / ¼ cup caster (superfine) sugar

1 large egg

55 g / 2 oz / ⅓ cup self-raising flour, sifted

2 tbsp cocoa powder

1 tbsp hazelnuts (cobnuts), finely chopped

1 tbsp chocolate hazelnut (cobnut) spread

TO DECORATE

30 g / 1 oz / ½ cup butter, softened

75 g / 2 ½ oz / ¾ cup icing (confectioner's) sugar

2 tsp cocoa powder, plus a little extra for sprinkling

1 tbsp hazelnuts (cobnuts), finely chopped

1. Beat the butter and sugar together in a mug until pale and smooth. Break the egg into a second mug and beat gently with a fork, then gradually stir the egg into the butter mixture. Fold in the flour and cocoa powder. Stir through the chopped hazelnut pieces and chocolate spread. Spoon half of the mixture into the mug used to beat the egg and level the tops.

2. Transfer the mugs to a microwave and cook on full power for 1 ½ minutes. Test the cakes by inserting a skewer into the centre – if it comes out clean, they're ready. If not, return to the microwave for 15 seconds and test again.

3. Leave the cakes to cool completely.

4. Beat the butter, icing sugar and cocoa powder until smooth and well whipped, adding a few drops of hot water if the mixture is too stiff.

5. Use a piping bag with a large star nozzle to pipe buttercream onto the cakes in a large swirl. Decorate with chopped hazelnuts and dust with cocoa powder.

Almond Mug Cake

30 g / 1 oz / ⅛ cup butter, softened

30 g / 1 oz / 1 ⅛ cup caster
  (superfine) sugar

1 medium egg

20 g / ¾ oz / ⅛ cup self-raising flour

2 tbsp ground almonds

1 tbsp milk

FOR THE FROSTING

1 tbsp icing (confectioner's) sugar

2 tsp water

1 tbsp almonds

1 tsp strawberry jam (jelly)

1. Mix the butter and sugar in a large mug. Add the egg and stir until well mixed.
2. Gradually stir in the flour and ground almonds. Add the milk and mix well.
3. Place the mug in the centre of the microwave and cook for 1 ½ minutes until well risen or until a skewer inserted in the centre comes out clean.
4. Place the icing sugar in a clean mug and gradually add the water and stir.
5. Pour the icing over the cake, decorate with whole almonds and the jam and serve.

Pumpkin and Ginger Mug Cakes

50 ml / 1 ¾ oz / ¼ cup sunflower oil

55 g / 2 oz / ¼ cup light muscovado sugar

75 g / 2 ½ oz / ½ cup self-raising
  flour, sifted

½ tsp ground ginger

50 g / 1 ¾ oz / ½ cup pumpkin or butternut
  squash, finely grated

1 tsp cocoa powder

1. Beat the oil and sugar together in a mug until pale and smooth.
2. Fold in the flour and ground ginger, followed by the pumpkin. Spoon half of the mixture into a second mug and level the tops.
3. Transfer the mugs to a microwave and cook on full power for 1 minute 30 seconds. Test the cakes by inserting a skewer into the centre – if it comes out clean, they are ready. If not, return to the microwave for 15 seconds and test again.
4. Sprinkle with a little cocoa and serve warm or at room temperature.

Chocolate Soufflé Mug Cakes

55 g / 2 oz / ¼ cup butter, softened
55 g / 2 oz / ¼ cup caster (superfine) sugar
1 large egg
55 g / 2 oz / ⅓ cup self-raising flour, sifted
2 tbsp unsweetened cocoa powder, plus extra for sprinkling
icing (confectioner's) sugar, for dusting

1. Beat the butter and sugar together in a mug until pale and smooth.
2. Break the egg into a second mug and beat gently with a fork, then gradually stir the egg into the butter mixture.
3. Fold in the flour and cocoa powder, then spoon half of the mixture into the mug you used to beat the egg and level the tops.
4. Transfer the mugs to a microwave and cook on full power for 1 minute 30 seconds. Test the cakes by inserting a skewer into the centre – if it comes out clean, they are ready. If not, return to the microwave for 15 seconds and test again.
5. Leave to rest for 1 minute, then dust the tops lightly with cocoa and icing sugar.
6. Delicious served with hot chocolate sauce (see Toppings chapter).

MAKES: **2** | PREP TIME: **15 MINS** | COOKING TIME: **1 MIN 30 SECS**

Dairy-free Heart Mug Cakes

55 g / 2 oz / ¼ cup dairy-free butter (or spread), softened

55 g / 2 oz / ¼ cup light muscovado sugar

1 large egg

1 tsp orange zest, finely grated

55 g / 2 oz / ⅓ cup self-raising flour, sifted

2 tbsp heart-shaped sugar confetti

1. Beat the dairy-free butter and sugar together in a mug until pale and smooth.

2. Break the egg into a second mug and add the orange zest. Beat gently with a fork, then gradually stir the egg into the butter mixture.

3. Fold in the flour and half the confetti, then spoon half of the mixture into the mug you used to beat the egg and level the tops. Sprinkle over the rest of the confetti.

4. Transfer the mugs to a microwave and cook on full power for 1 minute 30 seconds. Test the cakes by inserting a skewer into the centre – if it comes out clean, they're ready. If not, return to the microwave for 15 seconds and test again.

5. Leave the cakes to cool for 5 minutes before serving.

MAKES: 2 | PREP TIME: 30 MINS | COOKING TIME: 1 MIN 30 SECS

Toffee Coffee Mug Cakes

8 medjool dates, stoned and chopped

a pinch bicarbonate of (baking) soda

55 g / 2 oz / ¼ cup butter, softened

55 g / 2 oz / ¼ cup dark muscovado sugar

55 g / 2 oz / ⅓ cup self-raising flour, sifted

1 tsp instant espresso powder

1 large egg, beaten

TO DECORATE

30 g / 1 oz / ½ cup butter, softened

75 g / 2 ½ oz / ¾ cup icing (confectioner's) sugar

½ tsp instant espresso powder

1 tsp black treacle

1. Put the chopped dates in a mug with the bicarbonate of soda and 3 tablespoons of water.

2. Microwave for 45 seconds.

3. Add the butter and stir until melted, then beat in the sugar, flour, espresso powder and egg. Spoon half of the mixture into a second mug and level the tops.

4. Transfer the mugs to a microwave and cook on full power for 1 minute 30 seconds. Test the cakes by inserting a skewer into the centre – if it comes out clean, they're ready. If not, return to the microwave for 15 seconds and test again. Leave the cakes to cool completely.

5. Beat the butter, icing sugar, espresso powder and treacle together until pale and well whipped, adding a few drops of hot water if the mixture is too stiff.

6. Pipe a swirl of buttercream onto each cake using a piping bag fitted with a large star nozzle.

MAKES: 2 | PREP TIME: 15 MINS | COOKING TIME: 1 MIN 30 SECS

Chocolate Chunk Mug Cakes

55 g / 2 oz / ¼ cup butter, softened
55 g / 2 oz / ¼ cup caster (superfine) sugar
1 large egg
55 g / 2 oz / ⅓ cup self-raising flour, sifted
2 tbsp unsweetened cocoa powder
30 g / 1 oz / ⅕ cup milk chocolate, chopped, plus extra for grating over

1. Beat the butter and sugar together in a mug until pale and smooth.
2. Break the egg into a second mug and beat gently with a fork, then gradually stir the egg into the butter mixture.
3. Fold in the flour, cocoa powder and chopped chocolate, then spoon half of the mixture into the mug you used to beat the egg and level the tops.
4. Transfer the mugs to a microwave and cook on full power for 1 minute 30 seconds. Test the cakes by inserting a skewer into the centre – if it comes out clean, they are ready. If not, return to the microwave for 15 seconds and test again.
5. Leave to cool for 5 minutes, then grate over a little more chocolate.
6. Delicious served with vanilla custard (see Toppings chapter).

Fruity

MAKES: **2** | PREP TIME: **10 MINS** | COOKING TIME: **2 MINS**

Cocoa Cranberry Mug Cakes

55 g / 2 oz / ¼ cup butter, softened

55 g / 2 oz / ¼ cup caster (superfine) sugar

1 large egg

55 g / 2 oz / ⅓ cup self-raising flour, sifted

2 tbsp unsweetened cocoa powder, plus extra for sprinkling

1 tbsp dried cranberries

icing (confectioner's) sugar, for dusting

2 tsp cranberry jam (jelly)

1. Beat the butter and sugar together in a small mug until pale and smooth.

2. Break the egg into a second mug and beat gently with a fork, then gradually stir the egg into the butter mixture.

3. Fold in the flour, cocoa powder and dried cranberries, then spoon half of the mixture into the mug you used to beat the egg and level the tops.

4. Transfer the mugs to a microwave and cook on full power for 1 minute 30 seconds. Test the cakes by inserting a skewer into the centre – if it comes out clean, they're ready. If not, return to the microwave for 15 seconds and test again. Leave to cool for 5 minutes.

5. Leave to rest for 1 minute, then dust the tops lightly with icing sugar and add a spoonful of cranberry jam to each one.

MAKES: **2** | PREP TIME: **30 MINS** | COOKING TIME: **1 MIN 30 SECS**

Blueberry Mug Cakes

55 g / 2 oz / ¼ cup butter, softened
55 g / 2 oz / ¼ cup caster (superfine) sugar
1 large egg
1 tsp lemon zest, finely grated
55 g / 2 oz / ⅓ cup self-raising flour, sifted
1 handful blueberries
icing (confectioner's) sugar, for dusting

1. Beat the butter and sugar together in a mug until pale and smooth.
2. Break the egg into a second mug and add the lemon zest. Beat gently with a fork, then gradually stir the egg into the butter mixture.
3. Fold in the flour, then spoon half of the mixture into the mug you used to beat the egg. Push a few blueberries down into the centre of each one and level the tops.
4. Transfer the mugs to a microwave and cook on full power for 1 minute 30 seconds. Test the cakes by inserting a skewer into the centre – if it comes out clean, they are ready. If not, return to the microwave for 15 seconds and test again.
5. Leave the cakes to cool for 5 minutes. Dust lightly with icing sugar and garnish with the rest of the blueberries.

MAKES: 2 | PREP TIME: 15 MINS | COOKING TIME: 3 MINS

Strawberry Delight Mug Cake

50 g / 1 ¾ oz / ⅓ cup self-raising flour

a pinch of salt

3 egg whites

¼ tsp cream of tartar

65 g / 2 ⅓ oz / ⅓ cup caster (superfine) sugar

strawberries for garnish

1. Sieve the self-raising flour and salt together.
2. Using an electric whisk, whisk the egg whites in a clean bowl until foamy.
3. Add the cream of tartar and whisk for 1 minute.
4. Gradually add the sugar whilst whisking until all the sugar is incorporated and stiff peaks form.
5. Using a spatula, fold in the flour and salt, a little at a time, until well mixed and a smooth batter is formed.
6. Divide the mixture between two large mugs.
7. Place one of the mugs in the centre of the microwave and cook for 1 ½ minutes at 60% power.
8. Check the cake at 30 second intervals; a skewer should come out clean.
9. Place the second mug in the microwave and cook as before. Garnish with fresh strawberries.

Chocolate Orange Mug Cake

40 g / 1 ½ oz / ¼ cup self-raising flour
40 g / 1 ½ oz / ¼ cup caster
    (superfine) sugar
20 g / ¾ oz / ⅛ cup cocoa powder
1 medium egg
2 tbsp milk
2 tbsp vegetable oil
1 tbsp chocolate chips
zest of ½ small orange, reserving some
    as garnish

1. Mix the flour, sugar and cocoa in a large mug.
2. Add the egg and thoroughly mix.
3. Combine the milk and oil in another mug, then add to the batter and stir.
4. Fold in the chocolate chips and the orange zest.
5. Place the mug in the centre of the microwave and cook for 1 ½ minutes on full power.
6. Check the cake by placing a skewer into the centre of the cake, it should come out clean when fully cooked.
7. Garnish with the remaining zest and serve.

Raspberry Swirl Mug Cake

30 g / 1 oz / ⅛ cup butter, softened
30 g / 1 oz / ⅛ cup caster (superfine) sugar
1 medium egg
30 g / 1 oz / ⅛ cup self-raising flour
1 tbsp milk
1 tbsp freeze-dried raspberry pieces

FOR THE FROSTING
10 g / 1/3 oz / ⅛ cup butter, softened
20 g / ¾ oz / ¼ cup icing
    (confectioner's) sugar
1 tbsp raspberry jam (jelly), sieved

1. Mix the butter and sugar in a large mug. Add the egg and stir until well mixed.
2. Gradually stir in the flour, then add the milk and mix well.
3. Stir in the raspberries. Place the mug in the centre of the microwave and cook for 1 ½ minutes until well risen or until a skewer inserted in the centre comes out clean.
4. To make the frosting, combine the butter and icing sugar and mix well.
5. Gently fold in the raspberry jam, to create a swirl effect.
6. Pipe or spoon onto the cooled cake and sprinkle with more freeze-dried raspberry pieces, if desired.

Mini Fruit Mug Cake

55 g / 2 oz / ¼ cup butter, softened
55 g / 2 oz / ¼ cup dark muscovado sugar
1 large egg
1 tsp citrus peel, finely chopped
2 tsp raisins
55 g / 2 oz / ⅓ cup self-raising flour, sifted

TO DECORATE
6–8 tbsp caster (superfine) sugar
4–6 tbsp water
4 tbsp whole pistachios,
  shelled and unsalted
2 tbsp dried cranberries
16 hazelnuts (cobnuts), shelled
4 whole almonds

1. Preheat the oven to 160°C (140°C fan) / 350F / gas 4. Beat the butter and sugar together in an ovenproof mug. Break the egg into a second ovenproof mug. Beat with a fork, then gradually stir the egg into the butter mixture.
2. Fold in the peel, raisins and flour, mixing to combine. Spoon half of the mixture into the mug you used to beat the egg and level the tops. Transfer the mugs to a baking tray and cook in the oven for 16 minutes. Leave the cakes to cool completely.
3. Mix the sugar with the water over a medium heat until it has dissolved into a thick syrup. Brush the syrup over the tops of the cooled cakes. Arrange the nuts and dried fruit across the cakes and serve.

Chocolate and Blueberry Mug Cakes

55 g / 2 oz / ¼ cup butter, softened
55 g / 2 oz / ¼ cup caster (superfine) sugar
1 large egg
55 g / 2 oz / ⅓ cup self-raising flour, sifted
2 tbsp unsweetened cocoa powder
2 tbsp blueberry jam (jelly)

TO DECORATE
30 g / 1 oz / ½ cup butter, softened
75 g / 2 ½ oz / ¾ cup icing (confectioner's)
  sugar, plus extra for dusting
1 tbsp unsweetened cocoa powder

1. Beat the butter and sugar together in a mug until pale and smooth.
2. Break the egg into a second mug. Beat gently with a fork, then gradually stir the egg into the butter mixture. Fold in the flour and cocoa, then spoon half of the mixture into the mug you used to beat the egg. Level the tops, then add a spoonful of blueberry jam to each one.
3. Transfer the mugs to a microwave and cook on full power for 1 minute 30 seconds. Leave the cakes to cool completely.
4. Beat the butter, icing sugar and most of the cocoa together until well whipped. Spoon the buttercream into a piping bag fitted with a large star nozzle and pipe a big swirl on top of each cake. Sprinkle with cocoa and fresh blueberries, if desired.

MAKES: **2** | PREP TIME: **20 MINS** | COOKING TIME: **1 MIN 30 SECS**

Citrus Mug Cake

55 g / 2 oz / ¼ cup butter, softened
55 g / 2 oz / ¼ cup caster
  (superfine) sugar
1 large egg
1 tsp orange extract
55 g / 2 oz / ⅓ cup self-raising
  flour, sifted
½ lemon, zested
½ lime, zested

TO DECORATE
30 g / 1 oz / ½ cup butter, softened
75 g / 2 ½ oz / ¾ cup icing
  (confectioner's) sugar, plus extra
  for dusting
1 tsp orange extract
1 tsp green sugar balls

1. Beat the butter and sugar together in a mug until pale and smooth.
2. Break the egg into a second mug and add the orange extract. Beat gently with a fork, then gradually stir the egg into the butter mixture.
3. Fold in the flour and stir through the lemon and lime zest, then spoon half of the mixture into the mug you used to beat the egg and level the tops.
4. Transfer the mugs to a microwave and cook on full power for 1 ½ minutes. Test the cakes by inserting a skewer into the centre – if it comes out clean, they're ready. If not, return to the microwave for 15 seconds and test again. Leave the cakes to cool completely.
5. Beat the butter, icing sugar and orange extract together until pale and creamy, adding a few drops of hot water if the mixture is too stiff.
6. Spoon the buttercream into a piping bag fitted with a medium plain nozzle and pipe a spiral swirl on top of each cake.
7. Decorate with the green sugar balls.

Raspberry Pavlova Mug Cake

55 g / 2 oz / ¼ cup butter, softened
55 g / 2 oz / ¼ cup caster (superfine) sugar
1 large egg
55 g / 2 oz / ⅓ cup self-raising flour, sifted
2 tbsp fresh raspberries, chopped

TO DECORATE
250 ml / 9 fl. oz / 1 cup fresh whipping cream
6 fresh raspberries
2 mini meringues (see Toppings chapter
  for recipe)

1. Beat the butter and sugar together in a mug until pale and glossy.
2. Break the egg into a second mug. Beat gently with a fork, then gradually stir the egg into the butter mixture. Fold in the flour and the chopped fresh raspberries, then spoon half of the mixture into the mug you used to beat the egg and level the tops.
3. Put the mugs in a microwave and cook for 1 ½ minutes. Test the cakes by inserting a skewer into the centre – if it comes out clean, they're ready. If not, return to the microwave for 15 seconds and test again. Leave the cakes to cool completely.
4. Whip the cream with an electric whisk until it is light and fluffy, and holds its shape. It should be of piping consistency. Spoon the cream into a piping bag fitted with a small plain nozzle and pipe teardrops around the outsides of the cakes. Arrange the fresh raspberries in the centre and top with a mini meringue before serving.

Lemon Mug Cakes

65 g / 2 oz / ¼ cup butter, softened
50 g / 1 ¾ oz / ¼ cup caster (superfine)
  sugar, plus 2 tbsp
1 large egg
2 tbsp whole milk
1 lemon, juiced and zest finely pared
55 g / 2 oz / ⅓ cup self-raising flour, sifted
½ tbsp cornflour (cornstarch)
2 sprigs mint

1. Beat the butter and sugar together in a large mug until pale and smooth.
    Break the egg into a second large mug and add the milk and half of the lemon zest. Beat gently with a fork, then gradually stir the egg into the butter mixture.
2. Fold in the flour, then spoon half of the mixture into the mug you used to beat the egg and level the tops. Mix the rest of the lemon zest with 2 tablespoons of caster sugar and the cornflour and sprinkle it over the top of the cake mixture. Stir 200 ml of boiling water into the lemon juice, then spoon it over the cakes.
3. Transfer the mugs to a microwave and cook on full power for 2 minutes or until well risen and springy on top.
4. Leave the cakes to cool for a few minutes before serving, garnished with mint.

MAKES: **1** | PREP TIME: **5 MINS** | COOKING TIME: **2 MINS**

Summer Fruit Mug Cake

30 g / 1 oz / ⅛ cup butter, softened

30 g / 1 oz / ⅛ cup caster (superfine) sugar

1 medium egg

30 g / 1 oz / ⅛ cup self-raising flour

1 tbsp milk

1 tbsp frozen mixed berries (defrosted)

FOR THE TOPPING

1 tbsp frozen mixed berries (defrosted)

1 tbsp strawberry jam (jelly)

1. Mix the butter and sugar in a large mug.
2. Add the egg and stir until well mixed.
3. Gradually stir in the flour, then add the milk and mix well.
4. Fold in the mixed berries.
5. Place the mug in the centre of the microwave and cook for 1 ½ minutes until well risen or until a skewer inserted in the centre comes out clean. Allow to cool.
6. In a separate mug, combine the frozen berries and jam, then cook for 30 seconds.
7. Spoon the cooked berries onto the cake and serve.

MAKES: 2 | PREP TIME: 20 MINS | COOKING TIME: 1 MIN 30 SECS

Pineapple and Banana Mug Cake

55 g / 2 oz / ¼ cup butter, softened

55 g / 2 oz / ¼ cup caster (superfine) sugar

1 large egg

½ tsp vanilla extract

½ fresh banana, roughly mashed

2 tbsp canned pineapple chunks, drained and finely chopped

55 g / 2 oz / ⅓ cup self-raising flour, sifted

TO DECORATE

30 g / 1 oz / ½ cup butter, softened

75 g / 2 ½ oz / ¾ cup icing (confectioner's) sugar, plus extra for dusting

½ tsp vanilla extract

6 pieces of dried or candied pineapple

1. Beat the butter and sugar together in a mug until pale and smooth.
2. Break the egg into a second mug and add the vanilla extract. Beat gently with a fork, then gradually stir the egg into the butter mixture. Mix through the banana and pineapple pieces.
3. Fold in the flour, then spoon half of the mixture into the mug you used to beat the egg and level the tops.
4. Transfer the mugs to a microwave and cook on full power for 1 ½ minutes. Test the cakes by inserting a skewer into the centre – if it comes out clean, they're ready. If not, return to the microwave for 15 seconds and test again. Leave the cakes to cool completely.
5. Beat the butter, icing sugar and vanilla extract together until pale and creamy, adding a few drops of hot water if the mixture is too stiff.
6. Spoon the buttercream into a piping bag fitted with a small plain nozzle and pipe teardrops around top of each cake.
7. Top each cake with a few pieces of dried or candied pineapple and dust with icing sugar to serve.

MAKES: **2** | PREP TIME: **20 MINS** | COOKING TIME: **1 MIN 30 SECS**

Very Berry Mug Cake

55 g / 2 oz / ¼ cup butter, softened
55 g / 2 oz / ¼ cup caster (superfine) sugar
1 large egg
55 g / 2 oz / ⅓ cup self-raising flour, sifted
3 tbsp mixed berries, defrosted if frozen

TO DECORATE
30 g / 1 oz / ½ cup butter, softened
75 g / 2 ½ oz / ¾ cup icing (confectioner's) sugar, plus extra for dusting
2 tbsp mixed berries, defrosted if frozen

1. Beat the butter and sugar together in a mug until pale and smooth.
2. Break the egg into a second mug and beat gently with a fork, then gradually stir the egg into the butter mixture.
3. Fold in the flour, followed by the berries, then spoon half of the mixture into the mug you used to beat the egg and level the tops.
4. Transfer the mugs to a microwave and cook on full power for 1 ½ minutes. Test the cakes by inserting a skewer into the centre – if it comes out clean, they're ready. If not, return to the microwave for 15 seconds and test again. Leave the cakes to cool completely.
5. Beat the butter and icing sugar together until pale and well whipped, adding a few drops of hot water if the mixture is too stiff.
6. Spoon the buttercream into a piping bag fitted with a large star nozzle and pipe a big ring on top of each cake. Fill the centre of the rings with berries and serve immediately.

Apple and Berry Mug Cake

30 g / 1 oz / ⅛ cup butter, softened
30 g / 1 oz / ⅛ cup caster (superfine) sugar
1 medium egg
30 g / 1 oz / ⅛ cup self-raising flour
1 tbsp milk

FOR THE COMPOTE
½ apple, finely cubed
2 large strawberries, diced
1 small handful of blackberries
1 tbsp caster (superfine) sugar

1. In a microwaveable bowl, place the apple, strawberries and blackberries (reserving a few for garnish) and sugar and mix well.
2. Cook in the microwave for 2 minutes, stir and set aside to cool.
3. Mix the butter and sugar in a large mug.
4. Add the egg and stir until well mixed.
5. Gradually stir in the flour, then add the milk and mix well.
6. Stir in half of the apple and berry compote.
7. Place the mug in the centre of the microwave and cook for 1 ½ minutes until well risen or until a skewer inserted in the centre comes out clean.
8. Place the remaining fruit compote on top to serve.

MAKES: 2 | PREP TIME: 30 MINS | COOKING TIME: 1 MIN 30 SECS

Cherry and Berry Mug Cake

55 g / 2 oz / ¼ cup butter, softened
55 g / 2 oz / ¼ cup caster
   (superfine) sugar
1 large egg
55 g / 2 oz / ⅓ cup self-raising flour, sifted
3 tbsp chunky black cherry pie filling

TO DECORATE

30 g / 1 oz / ½ cup butter, softened
75 g / 2 ½ oz / ¾ cup icing
   (confectioner's) sugar
½ tsp vanilla extract
2 tbsp mixed berry jam (see Toppings
   chapter for recipe)

1. Beat the butter and sugar together in a mug until pale and smooth.
2. Break the egg into a second mug and beat gently with a fork, then gradually stir the egg into the butter mixture.
3. Fold in the flour and swirl in the cherry pie filling, then spoon half of the mixture into the mug you used to beat the egg and level the tops.
4. Transfer the mugs to a microwave and cook on full power for 1 ½ minutes. Test the cakes by inserting a skewer into the centre – if it comes out clean, they're ready. If not, return to the microwave for 15 seconds and test again. Leave the cakes to cool.
5. Beat the butter, icing sugar and vanilla extract together until pale and well whipped, adding a few drops of hot water if the mixture is too stiff.
6. Spoon the buttercream into a piping bag fitted with a small plain nozzle and pipe some teardrops around one side of each cake.
7. Spoon a mixed berry jam onto the top of the cake and serve.

MAKES: 2 | PREP TIME: 30 MINS | COOKING TIME: 1 MIN 30 SECS

Apple Crumble Mug Cake

55 g / 2 oz / ¼ cup butter, softened
55 g / 2 oz / ¼ cup caster
  (superfine) sugar
1 large egg
55 g / 2 oz / ⅓ cup self-raising flour, sifted
½ tsp ground cinnamon
1 small apple, peeled, cored and diced,
  4 slices reserved to garnish
1 handful raisin

FOR THE CRUMBLE
2 tbsp butter, diced
4 tbsp plain (all-purpose) flour
2 tbsp soft light brown sugar

1. Beat the butter and sugar together in a mug until pale and smooth.
2. Break the egg into a second mug and beat gently with a fork, then gradually stir the egg into the butter mixture.
3. Fold in the flour and ground cinnamon, followed by the apple and raisins, then spoon half of the mixture into the mug you used to beat the egg and level the tops.
4. To make the crumble topping, rub the butter into the flour, then stir in the sugar. Sprinkle it over the cake mixture in the mugs.
5. Transfer the mugs to a microwave and cook on full power for 1 ½ minutes. Test the cakes by inserting a skewer into the centre – if it comes out clean, they're ready. If not, return to the microwave for 15 seconds and test again.
6. Brown the crumble lightly under a hot grill and serve warm or at room temperature, topped with apple slices.

Coconut Lime Mug Cake

55 g / 2 oz / ¼ cup butter, softened
55 g / 2 oz / ¼ cup caster (superfine) sugar
1 large egg
½ tsp lime extract
55 g / 2 oz / ⅓ cup self-raising flour, sifted
4 tsp desiccated coconut

TO DECORATE
30 g / 1 oz / ½ cup butter, softened
75 g / 2 ½ oz / ¾ cup icing
   (confectioner's) sugar
½ tsp lime extract
2 tsp dried coconut pieces
½ lime, zested

1. Beat the butter and sugar together in a mug until pale and smooth. Break the egg into a second mug and add the lime extract. Beat gently with a fork, then gradually stir the egg into the butter mixture.

2. Fold in the flour and stir through the desiccated coconut, then spoon half of the mixture into the mug you used to beat the egg and level the tops.

3. Transfer the mugs to a microwave and cook on full power for 1 ½ minutes. Test the cakes by inserting a skewer into the centre – if it comes out clean, they are ready. If not, return to the microwave for 15 seconds and test again. Leave the cakes to cool completely.

4. Beat the butter, icing sugar and lime extract together until creamy, adding a few drops of hot water if the mixture is too stiff. Spoon the buttercream onto the top of each cake and smooth into a dome with the back of a spoon.

5. Top with the dried coconut pieces and sprinkle with lime zest before serving.

Vegan Apple Mug Cakes

2 tbsp dairy-free cream
2 tbsp coconut milk
½ tbsp sunflower oil
¼ lemon, juiced
50 g / 1 ¾ oz / ⅓ cup self-raising flour
2 tbsp caster (superfine) sugar
½ small eating apple, cored and chopped
2 tbsp icing (confectioner's) sugar

1. Mix 1 tablespoon of the dairy-free cream with the coconut milk, oil and lemon juice in a mug. Add the flour and caster sugar and stir, then fold in the chopped apple.

2. Transfer the mug to a microwave and cook on full power for 1 minute. Test the cake by inserting a skewer into the centre – if it comes out clean, it's ready. If not, return to the microwave for 10 seconds and test again.

3. Leave to cool for 5 minutes.

4. Mix the remaining tablespoon of dairy-free cream with the icing sugar and drizzle it over the top before serving.

MAKES: **1** | PREP TIME: **10 MINS** | COOKING TIME: **1 MIN 30 SECS**

Orange and Cranberry Mug Cake

30 g / 1 oz / ⅛ cup butter, softened

30 g / 1 oz / ⅛ cup caster (superfine) sugar

1 medium egg

30 g / 1 oz / ⅛ cup self-raising flour

1 tbsp milk

1 tbsp dried cranberries soaked in 1 tsp orange liqueur

zest of ½ orange

1 tbsp orange juice

TO DECORATE

1 tbsp dried cranberries soaked in 1 tsp orange liqueur

1 segment of satsuma

1. Mix the butter and sugar in a large mug.
2. Add the egg and stir until well mixed.
3. Gradually stir in the flour, then add the milk and mix well.
4. Fold in the soaked cranberries, orange zest and juice.
5. Place the mug in the centre of the microwave and cook for 1 ½ minutes until well risen or until a skewer inserted in the centre comes out clean.
6. Top with more soaked cranberries and the satsuma segment.

Fig and Pear Mug Cakes

55 g / 2 oz / ¼ cup butter, softened
55 g / 2 oz / ¼ cup caster (superfine) sugar
1 large egg
1 ½ tsp sirop de figue
55 g / 2 oz / ⅓ cup self-raising flour, sifted
2 dried figs, finely chopped
2 canned pear halves, finely diced

TO DECORATE
icing (confectioner's) sugar for dusting

1. Preheat the oven to 160°C (140°C fan) / 350F / gas 4. Beat the butter and sugar together in an ovenproof mug until pale and smooth.
2. Break the egg into a second ovenproof mug and add the sirop de figue. Beat gently with a fork, then gradually stir the egg into the butter mixture.
3. Fold in the flour, chopped figs and diced pears. Next, spoon half of the mixture into the mug you used to beat the egg and level the tops.
4. Transfer the mugs to a baking tray and cook in the centre of the oven for 16 minutes. Test the cakes by inserting a skewer into the centre – if it comes out clean, they're ready. If not, return to the oven for a couple of minutes and test again. Leave the cakes to cool a little.
5. Dust each cake with a little icing sugar before serving warm.
6. Vanilla custard makes an ideal topping for these mug cakes (see Toppings chapter).

Vegan Banana Mug Cake

1 very ripe banana, ½ mashed, ½ sliced
2 tbsp soya milk
1 tbsp sunflower oil
¼ tsp vanilla extract
50 g / 1 ¾ oz / ⅓ cup self-raising flour
2 tbsp caster (superfine) sugar

1. Whisk the mashed banana with the soya milk, oil and vanilla extract with a fork in a small mug. Add the flour and caster sugar and stir well, then level the surface.
2. Transfer the mug to a microwave and cook on full power for 1 minute 30 seconds. Test the cake by inserting a skewer into the centre – if it comes out clean, it's ready. If not, return to the microwave for 10 seconds and test again.
3. Leave to cool for 5 minutes, then top with the sliced banana and serve.

MAKES: 2 | PREP TIME: 30 MINS | COOKING TIME: 1 MIN 30 SECS

Apricot Mug Cake

55 g / 2 oz / ¼ cup butter, softened
55 g / 2 oz / ¼ cup caster (superfine) sugar
1 large egg
55 g / 2 oz / ⅓ cup self-raising flour, sifted
4 canned apricot halves, finely diced
1 tbsp apricot jam (jelly)

TO DECORATE
30 g / 1 oz / ½ cup butter, softened
75 g / 2 ½ oz / ¾ cup icing (confectioner's) sugar, plus extra for dusting
½ tsp vanilla extract
6 canned apricot halves

1. Beat the butter and sugar together in a mug until pale and smooth.
2. Break the egg into a second mug and beat gently with a fork, then gradually stir the egg into the butter mixture.
3. Fold in the flour, followed by the apricot pieces and jam, then spoon half of the mixture into the mug you used to beat the egg and level the tops.
4. Transfer the mugs to a microwave and cook on full power for 1 ½ minutes. Test the cakes by inserting a skewer into the centre – if it comes out clean, they're ready. If not, return to the microwave for 15 seconds and test again. Leave the cakes to cool completely.
5. Beat the butter and icing sugar and vanilla extract together until pale and creamy.
6. Spoon the buttercream into a piping bag fitted with a large plain nozzle and pipe a ring round the edge of each cake.
7. Fill the centre of each buttercream ring with the apricot halves.

Breakfast Mug Cakes

55 g / 2 oz / ¼ cup butter, softened
55 g / 2 oz / ¼ cup caster (superfine) sugar
1 large egg
55 g / 2 oz / ⅓ cup self-raising flour, sifted
1 tbsp raisins
1 tbsp apple juice
2 tbsp Greek yogurt
2 tbsp toasted oats
fresh fruit, to garnish

1. Beat the butter and sugar together in a mug until pale and smooth.
2. Break the egg into a second mug and beat gently with a fork, then gradually stir the egg into the butter mixture.
3. Fold in the flour, followed by the raisins and apple juice, then spoon half of the mixture into the mug you used to beat the egg and level the tops.
4. Transfer the mugs to a microwave and cook on full power for 1 minute 30 seconds. Test the cakes by inserting a skewer into the centre – if it comes out clean, they're ready. If not, return to the microwave for 15 seconds and test again.
5. Leave to cool for 5 minutes, then top with yogurt, toasted oats and fresh fruit.

Banana and Cinnamon Cream Mug Cakes

55 g / 2 oz / ¼ cup butter, softened
55 g / 2 oz / ¼ cup caster (superfine) sugar
1 small banana, peeled
1 large egg
55 g / 2 oz / ⅓ cup self-raising flour, sifted
1 tsp ground cinnamon, plus extra
for sprinkling
150 ml / 5 ½ fl. oz / ⅔ cup double
(heavy) cream

1. Beat the butter and sugar together in a mug until pale and smooth.
2. Mash the banana with a fork in a second mug, then break the egg and beat them gently together.
3. Gradually stir the banana mixture into the butter mixture, then fold in the flour and cinnamon. Spoon half of the mixture into the mug you used to mash the banana and level the tops.
4. Transfer the mugs to a microwave and cook on full power for 1 minute 30 seconds or until risen and the tops spring back when prodded. Leave to cool completely.
5. Whip the cream until it holds its shape, then spoon it into a piping bag fitted with a large star nozzle. Pipe a big swirl of cream on top of each cake and sprinkle with cinnamon.

MAKES: 2 | PREP TIME: 30 MINS | COOKING TIME: 1 MIN 30 SECS

Blackberry Cheesecake Mug Cake

55 g / 2 oz / ¼ cup butter, softened

55 g / 2 oz / ¼ cup caster (superfine) sugar

1 large egg

55 g / 2 oz / ⅓ cup self-raising flour, sifted

2 tbsp fresh blackberries, chopped

TO DECORATE

250 ml / 9 fl. oz / 1 cup fresh whipping cream

2 tbsp icing (confectioner's) sugar, plus extra for dusting

2 tbsp cream cheese

4–6 fresh blackberries

1. Beat the butter and sugar together in a mug until pale and shiny.
2. Break the egg into a second mug. Beat gently with a fork, then gradually stir the egg into the butter mixture.
3. Fold in the flour and the chopped blackberries, then spoon half of the mixture into the mug you used to beat the egg and level the tops.
4. Transfer the mugs to a microwave and cook on full power for 1 ½ minutes. Test the cakes by inserting a skewer into the centre – if it comes out clean, they're ready. If not, return to the microwave for 15 seconds and test again.
5. Leave the cakes to cool completely.
6. Whip the cream with an electric whisk until it holds its shape. It should be of piping consistency.
7. Mix the icing sugar with the cream cheese until combined. Spread a layer of the sweetened cheese onto the cake tops of the cakes and smooth with a palette knife.
8. Spoon the cream into a piping bag fitted with a medium plain nozzle and pipe a generous pillow of fresh cream on top of the cheese layer.
9. Arrange the fresh blackberries in the centre and dust with icing sugar before serving.

MAKES: **2** | PREP TIME: **30 MINS** | COOKING TIME: **1 MIN 30 SECS**

Apple and Cinnamon Cream Mug Cakes

55 g / 2 oz / ¼ cup butter, softened
55 g / 2 oz / ¼ cup caster (superfine) sugar
1 large egg
55 g / 2 oz / ⅓ cup self-raising flour, sifted
½ tsp ground cinnamon, plus extra for sprinkling
½ eating apple, peeled, cored and diced
150 ml / 5 ½ fl. oz / ⅔ cup double (heavy) cream

1. Beat the butter and sugar together in a mug until pale and smooth.
2. Break the egg into a second mug and beat gently with a fork, then gradually stir the egg into the butter mixture.
3. Fold in the flour and ground cinnamon, followed by the apple, then spoon half of the mixture into the mug you used to beat the egg and level the tops.
4. Transfer the mugs to a microwave and cook on full power for 1 minute 30 seconds. Test the cakes by inserting a skewer into the centre – if it comes out clean, they're ready. If not, return to the microwave for 15 seconds and test again. Leave to cool completely.
5. Whip the cream until it holds its shape, then spoon it into a piping bag fitted with a large star nozzle. Pipe a big swirl of cream on top of each cake and sprinkle with cinnamon.

MAKES: **2** | PREP TIME: **10 MINS** | COOKING TIME: **1 MIN 30 SECS**

Blueberry Custard Mug Cakes

55 g / 2 oz / ¼ cup butter, softened

55 g / 2 oz / ¼ cup caster (superfine) sugar, plus extra for sprinkling

2 tbsp custard powder

75 ml / 2 ½ fl. oz / ⅓ cup whole milk

55 g / 2 oz / ⅓ cup self-raising flour, sifted

1 handful blueberries

1. Beat the butter and sugar together in a mug until pale and smooth.
2. Whisk the mustard powder and milk together in a second mug until smooth, then beat it into the butter mixture.
3. Fold in the flour and blueberries, then spoon half of the mixture into the mug you mixed the custard in and level the tops.
4. Transfer the mugs to a microwave and cook on full power for 1 minute 30 seconds. Test the cakes by inserting a skewer into the centre – if it comes out clean, they are ready. If not, return to the microwave for 15 seconds and test again.
5. Leave the cakes to cool for 5 minutes before serving, sprinkled with caster sugar.

MAKES: **1** | PREP TIME: **15 MINS** | COOKING TIME: **1 MIN**

Sour Cream and Raspberry Mug Cake

2 tbsp sour cream

2 tbsp whole milk

½ tbsp sunflower oil

¼ lemon, juiced

50 g / 1 ¾ oz / ⅓ cup self-raising flour

2 tbsp caster (superfine) sugar

5 fresh raspberries

2 tbsp icing (confectioner's) sugar

1. Mix 1 tablespoon of the sour cream with the milk, oil and lemon juice in a small mug. Add the flour and caster sugar and stir well, then poke the raspberries into the mixture.
2. Transfer the mug to a microwave and cook on full power for 1 minute. Test the cake by inserting a skewer into the centre – if it comes out clean, it's ready. If not, return to the microwave for 10 seconds and test again.
3. Leave to cool for 5 minutes.
4. Mix the remaining 1 tablespoon of sour cream with the icing sugar and drizzle it over the top before serving.

Indulgent

MAKES: 1 | PREP TIME: 5 MINS | COOKING TIME: 5 MINS

Salted Caramel Mug Cake

30 g / 1 oz / ⅛ cup butter

30 g / 1 oz / ⅛ cup caster (superfine) sugar

1 tsp vanilla extract

1 medium egg

30 g / 1 oz / ⅛ cup self-raising flour

1 tbsp milk

FOR THE CARAMEL SAUCE

2 tbsp caster (superfine) sugar

1 tbsp boiling water

2 tsp salted butter

1 tbsp double (heavy) cream

a pinch of salt

1. Mix the butter, sugar and vanilla extract in a large mug.
2. Add the egg and stir until well mixed.
3. Gradually stir in the flour, then add the milk and mix well.
4. Place the mug in the centre of the microwave and cook for 1 ½ minutes until well risen or until a skewer inserted in the centre comes out clean.
5. For the caramel, combine the sugar and water in a clean mug.
6. Cook in the microwave for up to 3 minutes or until the sugar has started to caramelize and turn golden brown.
7. Immediately add the butter, cream and salt and then stir carefully but quickly to combine.
8. Pour over the sponge and serve.

MAKES: 1 | PREP TIME: 5 MINS | COOKING TIME: 1 MIN 30 SECS

Vanilla Fudge Mug Cake

30 g / 1 oz / ⅛ cup butter, softened
30 g / 1 oz / ⅛ cup caster (superfine) sugar
1 medium egg
30 g / 1 oz / ⅛ cup self-raising flour
1 tbsp milk
1 tsp vanilla extract
2 tbsp fudge pieces (see Toppings chapter for recipe)

1. Mix the butter and sugar in a large mug.
2. Add the egg and stir until well mixed.
3. Gradually stir in the flour and add the milk and vanilla extract; mix well.
4. Fold in the fudge pieces.
5. Place the mug in the centre of the microwave and cook for 1 ½ minutes until well risen or until a skewer inserted in the centre comes out clean.

Gooey Chocolate Cream Mug Cake

55 g / 2 oz / ¼ cup butter, softened
55 g / 2 oz / ¼ cup caster (superfine) sugar
1 large egg
55 g / 2 oz / ⅓ cup self-raising flour, sifted
2 tbsp cocoa powder
2 chocolate truffles

TO DECORATE
125 ml / 4 ½ fl. oz / ½ cup double (heavy) cream
cocoa powder for sprinkling

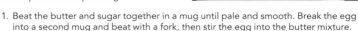

1. Beat the butter and sugar together in a mug until pale and smooth. Break the egg into a second mug and beat with a fork, then stir the egg into the butter mixture.
2. Fold in the flour and cocoa powder, then spoon half of the mixture into the mug you used to beat the egg. Press a chocolate truffle down into the centre of each cake and level the tops.
3. Transfer the mugs to a microwave and cook on full power for 1 ½ minutes or until the cake is well risen.
4. Leave the cakes to cool for 10 minutes while you prepare the cream. Whip the cream with an electric whisk until it holds its shape, then spoon it into a piping bag fitted with a large star nozzle. Pipe a swirl of cream on top of each cake, then sprinkle with cocoa powder and serve immediately.

Valentine's Mug Cakes

55 g / 2 oz / ¼ cup butter, softened
55 g / 2 oz / ¼ cup caster (superfine) sugar
1 large egg
2 tsp red food colouring
55 g / 2 oz / ⅓ cup self-raising flour, sifted
1 tbsp unsweetened cocoa powder
½ tsp ground cinnamon
1 tbsp heart-shaped sugar confetti

1. Beat the butter and sugar together in a mug until pale and smooth.
2. Break the egg into a second mug and add the food colouring. Beat together gently with a fork, then gradually stir the egg into the butter mixture.
3. Fold in the flour, cocoa and cinnamon. Spoon half of the mixture into the mug you used to beat the egg and level the tops.
4. Transfer the mugs to a microwave and cook on full power for 1 minute 30 seconds. Test the cakes by inserting a skewer into the centre – if it comes out clean, they are ready. If not, return to the microwave for 15 seconds and test again.
5. Leave to cool for 5 minutes, then garnish with sugar confetti.

MAKES: **1** | PREP TIME: **15 MINS** | COOKING TIME: **2 MINS**

Passion Fruit Mug Cake

30 g / 1 oz / ⅛ cup butter, softened

30 g / 1 oz / ⅛ cup caster (superfine) sugar

1 medium egg

30 g / 1 oz / ⅛ cup self-raising flour

1 tbsp milk

1 tbsp white chocolate chips

seeds and flesh of ½ passion fruit

FOR THE FROSTING

20 g / ¾ oz / ¼ cup icing (confectioner's) sugar

10 g soft butter

1 tbsp grated white chocolate

1. Mix the butter and sugar in a large mug.
2. Add the egg and stir until well mixed.
3. Gradually stir in the flour, then add the milk and mix well.
4. Stir in the chocolate chips and half of the passion fruit seeds.
5. Place the mug in the centre of the microwave and cook for 1 ½ minutes until well risen or until a skewer inserted in the centre comes out clean. Allow to cool.
6. To make the topping, combine the icing sugar and butter and mix until light and fluffy.
7. Melt the white chocolate for 20 seconds in the microwave.
8. Fold the melted white chocolate and remaining passion fruit into the frosting.
9. Spoon the frosting onto the top of the cake and serve.

MAKES: 4 | **PREP TIME: 15 MINS** | **COOKING TIME: 8–10 MINS**

Sticky Toffee Mug Cake

90 g / 3 ¼ oz / ½ cup finely chopped, pitted dates, plus 4 whole dates to serve

90 ml / 3 fl. oz / ⅓ cup boiling water

40 g / 1 ½ oz / ¼ cup butter, softened

75 g / 2 ½ oz / ½ cup dark brown sugar

1 medium egg

90 g / 3 ¼ oz / ½ cup self-raising flour

½ tsp bicarbonate of (baking) soda

FOR THE TOFFEE SAUCE

2 tbsp dark brown sugar

2 tsp boiling water

1 tbsp double (heavy) cream

1. Soak the finely-chopped dates in the boiling water for 5 minutes.
2. Cook in the microwave for 2 minutes.
3. Liquidize or mash the dates with a fork and set aside.
4. In a bowl, mix the butter and the sugar and whisk until light and fluffy.
5. Add the egg and whisk further.
6. Add the flour and bicarbonate of soda. Gently fold in the date mixture.
7. Divide between the 4 mugs.
8. Place each mug in the centre of the microwave and cook for 1 ½ minutes or until a skewer inserted in the centre comes out clean.
9. To make the toffee sauce, stir the sugar and water in another mug and cook for 3 minutes. Stir in the cream and pour over the cooked cakes.

MAKES: **1** | PREP TIME: **5 MINS** | COOKING TIME: **1 MIN 30 SECS**

Pistachio Mug Cake

30 g / 1 oz / ⅛ cup butter, softened
30 g / 1 oz / ⅛ cup caster (superfine) sugar
1 tsp green food dye
1 medium egg
20 g self-raising flour
2 tbsp ground pistachios
1 tbsp milk

TO DECORATE
icing (confectioner's) sugar to sprinkle
1 whole pistachio nut

1. Mix the butter, sugar and food dye in a large mug.
2. Add the egg and stir until well mixed.
3. Gradually stir in the flour and ground pistachios. Add the milk, then mix well.
4. Place the mug in the centre of the microwave and cook for 1 ½ minutes until well risen or until a skewer inserted in the centre comes out clean.
5. Dust with icing sugar and top with the whole pistachio nut.

MAKES: **2** | PREP TIME: **30 MINS** | COOKING TIME: **1 MIN 30 SECS**

Chocolate Espresso Mug Cake

55 g / 2 oz / ¼ cup butter, softened
55 g / 2 oz / ¼ cup caster (superfine) sugar
1 large egg
55 g / 2 oz / ⅓ cup self-raising flour, sifted
1 tsp instant espresso powder
1 tbsp cocoa powder

TO DECORATE
30 g / 1 oz / ½ cup butter, softened
75 g / 2 ½ oz / ¾ cup icing (confectioner's) sugar
½ tsp instant espresso powder

1. Beat the butter and sugar together in a mug until pale and smooth.
2. Break the egg into a second mug and beat gently with a fork, then gradually stir the egg into the butter mixture.
3. Fold in the flour, espresso powder and cocoa powder. Spoon half of the mixture into the mug you used to beat the egg and level the tops.
4. Transfer the mugs to a microwave and cook on full power for 1 ½ minutes. Test the cakes by inserting a skewer into the centre – if it comes out clean, the cakes are ready. If not, return to the microwave for 15 seconds and test again. Leave the cakes to cool completely.
5. Beat the butter, icing sugar and espresso powder together until pale and well whipped, adding a few drops of hot water if the mixture is too stiff. Spoon or pipe the buttercream onto the cakes and dust with cocoa powder.

Peanut Butter and Jam Mug Cake

55 g / 2 oz / ¼ cup butter, softened
55 g / 2 oz / ¼ cup caster (superfine) sugar
1 large egg
55 g / 2 oz / ⅓ cup self-raising flour, sifted
1 tbsp peanut butter
1 tbsp strawberry jam (jelly)

TO DECORATE
30 g / 1 oz / ½ cup butter, softened
75 g / 2 ½ oz / ¾ cup icing (confectioner's)
   sugar, plus extra for dusting
2 tbsp peanut butter
1 tbsp strawberry jam (jelly)

1. Beat the butter and sugar together in a mug until pale and smooth. Break the egg into a second mug and beat with a fork, then stir the egg into the butter mixture.
2. Fold in the flour, followed by the peanut butter and jam, then spoon half of the mixture into the mug you used to beat the egg and level the tops.
3. Transfer the mugs to a microwave and cook on full power for 1 ½ minutes. Test the cakes by inserting a skewer into the centre – if it comes out clean, the cakes are ready. If not, return to the microwave for 15 seconds and test again. Leave the cakes to cool completely.
4. Beat the butter, icing sugar and peanut butter together until pale and well whipped. Spoon the buttercream into a piping bag fitted with a large star nozzle and pipe a double ring round the edge of each cake. Fill the centre of each buttercream ring with strawberry jam.

Cinnamon Cake

30 g / 1 oz / ⅛ cup butter, softened
30 g / 1 oz / ⅛ cup caster (superfine) sugar
1 tsp ground cinnamon
1 medium egg
30 g self-raising flour
1 tbsp milk

FOR THE TOPPING
1 tbsp caster (superfine) sugar
1 tsp boiling water
½ tsp ground cinnamon
20 g / ¾ oz / ¼ cup icing
   (confectioner's) sugar
10 g / ⅓ oz / ⅛ cup soft butter

1. Mix the butter, sugar and cinnamon in a mug. Then stir in the egg, flour and milk.
2. Place the mug in the microwave and cook for 1 ½ minutes until risen. Set aside.
3. In another mug, combine the caster sugar, water and cinnamon. Cook in the microwave for 2 minutes and then allow to cool.
4. To make the frosting, combine the icing sugar and butter to make the buttercream.
5. Pipe the buttercream onto the cake and then drizzle over the cinnamon syrup.

MAKES: **2** | PREP TIME: **30 MINS** | COOKING TIME: **1 MIN 30 SECS**

Cookies and Cream Mug Cake

55 g / 2 oz / ¼ cup butter, softened
55 g / 2 oz / ¼ cup caster (superfine) sugar
1 large egg
55 g / 2 oz / ⅓ cup self-raising flour, sifted
4 mini chocolate cookies, roughly chopped

TO DECORATE
30 g / 1 oz / ½ cup butter, softened
75 g / 2 ½ oz / ¾ cup icing (confectioner's) sugar, plus extra for dusting
½ tsp vanilla extract
4 mini chocolate cookies

1. Beat the butter and sugar together in a mug until pale and smooth.
2. Break the egg into a second mug and beat gently with a fork, then gradually stir the egg into the butter mixture.
3. Fold in the flour, followed by the chopped cookies, and then spoon half of the mixture into the mug you used to beat the egg and level the tops.
4. Transfer the mugs to a microwave and cook on full power for 1 ½ minutes. Test the cakes by inserting a skewer into the centre – if it comes out clean, the cakes are ready. If not, return to the microwave for 15 seconds and test again. Leave the cakes to cool completely.
5. Beat the butter, icing sugar and vanilla extract together until pale and well whipped, adding a few drops of hot water if the mixture is too stiff.
6. Spoon the buttercream into a piping bag and pipe a big swirl on top of each cake.
7. Crumble two of the cookies into crumbs and sprinkle on top before garnishing each cake with a whole cookie.

MAKES: **2** | PREP TIME: **30 MINS** | COOKING TIME: **1 MIN 30 SECS**

Marshmallow Surprise Mug Cake

55 g / 2 oz / ¼ cup butter, softened
55 g / 2 oz / ¼ cup caster (superfine) sugar
1 large egg
½ tsp vanilla extract
55 g / 2 oz / ⅓ cup self-raising flour, sifted
2 tbsp mini marshmallows

TO DECORATE
30 g / 1 oz / ½ cup butter, softened
75 g / 2 ½ oz / ¾ cup icing (confectioner's)
   sugar, plus extra for dusting
2–4 large marshmallow twirls

1. Beat the butter and sugar together in a mug until pale and creamy.
2. Break the egg into a second mug and add the vanilla extract. Beat gently with a fork, then gradually stir the egg into the butter mixture.
3. Fold in the flour and the mini marshmallows, then spoon half of the mixture into the mug you used to beat the egg and level the tops.
4. Transfer the mugs to a microwave and cook on full power for 1 ½ minutes. Test the cakes by inserting a skewer into the centre – if it comes out clean, they're ready. If not, return to the microwave for 15 seconds and test again. Leave the cakes to cool completely.
5. Beat the butter and icing sugar together until well whipped, adding a few drops of hot water if the mixture is too stiff.
6. Spoon the buttercream into a piping bag fitted with a large plain nozzle and pipe a big swirl on top of each cake. Stick a marshmallow twirl into the top of each swirl and dust lightly with icing sugar.

MAKES: **1** | PREP TIME: **5 MINS** | COOKING TIME: **1 MIN 30 SECS**

Banoffee Mug Cake

30 g / 1 oz / ⅛ cup butter, softened
30 g / 1 oz / ⅛ cup caster (superfine) sugar
1 medium egg
30 g / 1 oz / ⅛ cup self-raising flour
1 tbsp milk
½ banana, mashed

TO DECORATE
½ banana, sliced
2 tbsp toffee sauce

1. Mix the butter and sugar in a large mug.
2. Add the egg and stir until well mixed.
3. Gradually stir in the flour, then add the milk and mix well.
4. Stir in the mashed banana.
5. Place the mug in the centre of the microwave and cook for 1 ½ minutes until well risen or until a skewer inserted in the centre comes out clean.
6. Decorate with slices of banana and drizzle with toffee sauce.

MAKES: 1 | PREP TIME: 10 MINS | COOKING TIME: 1 MIN 30 SECS

Red Velvet Mug Cake

30 g / 1 oz / ⅛ cup butter, softened

30 g / 1 oz / ⅛ cup caster (superfine) sugar

1 medium egg

1 tbsp milk

1 tbsp red food dye

30 g / 1 oz / ⅛ cup self-raising flour

20 g cocoa powder

FOR THE FROSTING

20 g cream cheese

20 g icing (confectioner's) sugar

red sugar sprinkles

1. Mix the butter and sugar in a large mug.
2. Add the egg and stir until well mixed.
3. In a separate mug combine the milk and food dye.
4. Gradually stir in the flour and cocoa powder and add the milk; mix well.
5. Place the mug in the centre of the microwave and cook for 1 ½ minutes until the cake is well risen or a skewer inserted in the centre comes out clean.
6. To make the frosting, combine the cream cheese and icing sugar.
7. Top the cooled cake with the frosting and sugar sprinkles and serve.

MAKES: 2 | **PREP TIME: 35 MINS** | **COOKING TIME: 1 MIN 30 SECS**

Rocky Road Mug Cake

55 g / 2 oz / ¼ cup butter, softened
55 g / 2 oz / ¼ cup caster (superfine) sugar
1 large egg
55 g / 2 oz / ⅓ cup self-raising flour, sifted
1 tbsp cocoa powder
1 tbsp dried cranberries
1 tbsp milk chocolate chunks
1 tbsp chopped mixed nuts

TO DECORATE
30 g / 1 oz / ½ cup butter, softened
75 g / 2 ½ oz / ¾ cup icing
    (confectioner's) sugar, plus extra
    for dusting
1 tbsp cocoa powder
6 tbsp milk chocolate chunks
8 marshmallows

1. Beat the butter and sugar together in a mug until pale and smooth.
2. Break the egg into a second mug and beat gently with a fork, then gradually stir the egg into the butter mixture.
3. Fold in the flour and cocoa powder, followed by the cranberries, chocolate chunks and nuts. Spoon half of the mixture into the mug you used to beat the egg and level the tops.
4. Transfer the mugs to a microwave and cook on full power for 1 ½ minutes. Test the cakes by inserting a skewer into the centre – if it comes out clean, the cakes are ready. If not, return to the microwave for 15 seconds and test again. Leave the cakes to cool completely.
5. Beat the butter, icing sugar and cocoa together until pale and well whipped, adding a few drops of hot water if the mixture is too stiff.
6. Spoon the buttercream onto the cakes and top with 2 tablespoons of the chocolate chunks and the marshmallows.
7. Put the rest of the chocolate chunks in a mug. Melt in the microwave on medium in 5 second bursts until melted, stirring in between.
8. Drizzle over the cakes and dust with icing sugar.

MAKES: 1 | PREP TIME: 5 MINS | COOKING TIME: 1 MIN 30 SECS

Black Forest Mug Cake

40 g / 1 ½ oz / ¼ cup self-raising flour
40 g / 1 ½ oz / ¼ cup caster (superfine) sugar
20 g cocoa powder
1 medium egg
2 tbsp milk
2 tbsp vegetable oil
1 tbsp chocolate chips
1 tbsp canned pitted black cherries
1 tbsp kirsch or cherry liqueur

1. Mix the flour, sugar and cocoa powder in a large mug.
2. Add the egg and thoroughly mix.
3. Combine the milk and oil in another mug, then add to the batter and stir.
4. Fold in the chocolate chips, cherries and liqueur.
5. Place the mug in the centre of the microwave and cook for 1 ½ minutes on full power.
6. Check the cake by placing a skewer into the centre of the cake, it should come out clean when fully cooked.

White Chocolate and Raspberry Mug Cake

30 g / 1 oz / ⅛ cup butter, softened
30 g / 1 oz / ⅛ cup caster (superfine) sugar
1 medium egg
30 g / 1 oz / ⅛ cup self-raising flour
1 tbsp milk
1 tbsp white chocolate chips
1 tbsp freeze-dried raspberry pieces

TO DECORATE
1 tbsp white chocolate
fresh raspberries

1. Mix the butter and sugar in a large mug. Add the egg and stir until well mixed.
2. Gradually stir in the flour, then add the milk and mix well. Then fold in the chocolate chips and the freeze-dried raspberry pieces.
3. Place the mug in the centre of the microwave and cook for 1 ½ minutes until well risen or until a skewer inserted in the centre comes out clean.
4. Melt the white chocolate for 20 seconds in the microwave. Decorate with fresh raspberries and melted white chocolate.

Malted Chocolate Mug Cakes

55 g / 2 oz / ¼ cup butter, softened
55 g / 2 oz / ¼ cup caster (superfine) sugar
1 large egg
55 g / 2 oz / ⅓ cup self-raising flour, sifted
1 tbsp cocoa powder

TO DECORATE
4 tbsp chocolate spread
1 small packet of malted chocolate balls
1 tbsp cocoa powder plus extra for dusting

1. Preheat the oven to 160°C (140°C fan) / 350F / gas 4.
2. Beat the butter and sugar together in an ovenproof mug until pale and smooth.
3. Break the egg into a second ovenproof mug and beat gently with a fork, then gradually stir the egg into the butter mixture.
4. Fold in the flour and cocoa powder and mix well to combine. Spoon half of the mixture into the mug you used to beat the egg and level the tops.
5. Transfer the mugs to a baking tray and cook in the centre of the oven for 16 minutes. Test the cakes by inserting a skewer into the centre – if it comes out clean, they're ready. If not, return to the oven for a couple of minutes and test again. Leave the cakes to cool completely.
6. Spread the tops of the cakes with the chocolate spread.
7. Cover the tops with malted chocolate balls and dust with cocoa powder.

MAKES: **2** | PREP TIME: **30 MINS** | COOKING TIME: **1 MIN 30 SECS**

Walnut Mocha Mug Cakes

55 g / 2 oz / ¼ cup butter, softened
55 g / 2 oz / ¼ cup caster
  (superfine) sugar
1 large egg
55 g / 2 oz / ⅓ cup self-raising flour, sifted
1 tsp instant espresso powder
1 tbsp unsweetened cocoa powder
1 tbsp walnuts, chopped

TO DECORATE
1 tbsp golden syrup
1 tbsp dark muscovado sugar
1 ½ tbsp butter
1 tsp unsweetened cocoa powder
1 tbsp walnuts, chopped

1. Beat the butter and sugar together in a mug until pale and smooth.
2. Break the egg into a second mug and beat gently with a fork, then gradually stir the egg into the butter mixture.
3. Fold in the flour, espresso powder, cocoa and walnuts. Spoon half of the mixture into the mug you used to beat the egg and level the tops.
4. Transfer the mugs to a microwave and cook on full power for 1 minute 30 seconds. Test the cakes by inserting a skewer into the centre – if it comes out clean, they're ready. If not, return to the microwave for 15 seconds and test again.
5. Put the golden syrup, muscovado sugar, butter and cocoa in a small bowl and microwave for 20 seconds, stirring halfway through.
6. Spoon the sauce over the cakes and decorate with chopped walnuts. Leave to cool for 5 minutes before serving.

MAKES: **2** | PREP TIME: **25 MINS** | COOKING TIME: **1 MIN 30 SECS**

Chocolate and Almond Mug Cakes

55 g / 2 oz / ¼ cup butter, softened
55 g / 2 oz / ¼ cup light muscovado sugar
1 large egg
½ tsp almond extract
55 g / 2 oz / ⅓ cup self-raising flour, sifted
2 tbsp unsweetened cocoa powder
1 tbsp ground almonds
icing (confectioner's) sugar, for dusting
150 ml / 5 ½ fl. oz / ⅔ cup double (heavy) cream
1 tbsp almonds, chopped

1. Beat the butter and sugar together in a mug until pale and smooth.
2. Break the egg into a second mug and add the almond extract. Beat gently with a fork, then gradually stir the egg into the butter mixture.
3. Fold in the flour, cocoa and ground almonds, then spoon half of the mixture into the mug you used to beat the egg and level the tops.
4. Transfer the mugs to a microwave and cook on full power for 1 minute 30 seconds or until well risen and the tops spring back when prodded. Leave to cool completely, then dust lightly with icing sugar.
5. Whip the cream until it holds its shape, then spoon it onto the cakes and sprinkle with chopped almonds.

Caffè Latte Mug Cake

55 g / 2 oz / ¼ cup butter, softened
55 g / 2 oz / ¼ cup caster (superfine) sugar
1 large egg
2 tbsp sweetened coffee and chicory essence
55 g / 2 oz / ⅓ cup self-raising flour, sifted

TO DECORATE
30 g / 1 oz / ½ cup butter, softened
½ tsp vanilla extract
75 g / 2 ½ oz / ¾ cup icing
  (confectioner's) sugar
2 chocolate-covered coffee beans

1. Beat the butter and sugar together in a mug until pale and silky. Break the egg into a second mug and beat gently with a fork and combine with the coffee essence, then gradually stir the egg mixture into the butter mixture.
2. Fold in the flour and combine well. Spoon half of the mixture into the mug you used to beat the egg and level the tops.
3. Transfer the mugs to a microwave and cook on full power for 1 ½ minutes. Test the cakes by inserting a skewer into the centre – if it comes out clean, they're ready. If not, return to the microwave for 15 seconds and test again. Leave the cakes to cool completely.
4. Beat the butter, vanilla extract and icing sugar until pale and well whipped, adding a few drops of hot water if the mixture is too stiff.
5. Put the buttercream into a piping bag with a small plain nozzle and pipe teardrops onto the tops of each cake.
6. Top with a chocolate-covered coffee bean.

Melt-in-the-middle Caramel Mug Cake

55 g / 2 oz / ¼ cup butter, softened
55 g / 2 oz / ¼ cup caster (superfine) sugar
1 large egg
55 g / 2 oz / ⅓ cup self-raising flour, sifted
1 ½ tbsp cocoa powder
6 squares caramel chocolate bar

1. Beat the butter and sugar together in a mug until pale and smooth.
2. Break the egg into a second mug and beat gently with a fork, then gradually stir the egg into the butter mixture.
3. Fold in the flour and cocoa powder, then spoon half of the mixture into the mug you used to beat the egg. Press 3 squares of the chocolate down into the centre of each cake and level the tops.
4. Transfer the mugs to a microwave and cook on full power for 1 ½ minutes or until well risen. Leave the cakes to stand for 5 minutes before serving.

Blue Lava Mug Cakes

55 g / 2 oz / ¼ cup butter, softened
55 g / 2 oz / ¼ cup caster (superfine) sugar
1 large egg
55 g / 2 oz / ⅓ cup self-raising flour, sifted
2 tbsp unsweetened cocoa powder, plus extra for sprinkling
30 g / 1 oz / ⅕ cup dark chocolate (minimum 60% cocoa solids), broken into chunks
2 tbsp icing (confectioner's) sugar
a few drops blue food colouring
1 tbsp multi-coloured sugar strands

1. Beat the butter and sugar together in a mug until pale and smooth.
2. Break the egg into a second mug and beat gently with a fork, then gradually stir the egg into the butter mixture.
3. Fold in the flour and cocoa powder, then spoon half of the mixture into the mug you used to beat the egg and level the tops. Arrange the chocolate chunks in the centre of each cake, then spoon ½ a tablespoon of water on top of each one.
4. Transfer the mugs to a microwave and cook on full power for 2 minutes.
5. Mix the icing sugar with just enough water to make a spoonable icing and colour it blue.
6. Use a small round cutter to remove a section from the top of each cake, revealing the molten centre below. Drizzle the icing over the cakes and decorate with sugar strands.
7. If desired, place some flavoured marshmallows in the centre to melt into the cake (see Toppings chapter for marshmallow recipe).

MAKES: 2 | PREP TIME: 30 MINS | COOKING TIME: 1 MIN 30 SECS

Toffee Waffle Cream Mug Cakes

55 g / 2 oz / ¼ cup butter, softened
55 g / 2 oz / ¼ cup light
   muscovado sugar
1 large egg
55 g / 2 oz / ⅓ cup self-raising flour, sifted
1 tsp ground cinnamon
150 ml / 5 ½ fl. oz / ⅔ cup double
   (heavy) cream
1 tbsp chocolate sauce
1 tbsp caramel sauce
1 toffee waffle, diced

1. Beat the butter and sugar together in a mug until pale and smooth.

2. Break the egg into a second mug and beat gently with a fork, then gradually stir the egg into the butter mixture.

3. Fold in the flour and cinnamon, then spoon half of the mixture into the mug you used to beat the egg and level the tops.

4. Transfer the mugs to a microwave and cook on full power for 1 minute 30 seconds or until well risen and the tops spring back when prodded. Leave to cool completely.

5. Whip the cream until it holds its shape, then spoon it into a piping bag fitted with a large star nozzle. Pipe a big swirl of cream on top of each cake.

6. Drizzle with the sauces and scatter over the waffle pieces.

MAKES: 2 | PREP TIME: 15 MINS | COOKING TIME: 1 MIN 30 SECS

Chai Latte Mug Cakes

55 g / 2 oz / ¼ cup butter, softened
55 g / 2 oz / ¼ cup light muscovado sugar
1 large egg
55 g / 2 oz / ⅓ cup self-raising flour, sifted
2 tsp chai latte powder
icing (confectioner's) sugar, for dusting

1. Beat the butter and sugar together in a mug until pale and smooth.
2. Break the egg into a second mug and beat it gently with a fork, then gradually stir the egg into the butter mixture.
3. Fold in the flour and chai powder, then spoon half of the mixture into the mug you used to beat the egg and level the tops.
4. Transfer the mugs to a microwave and cook on full power for 1 minute 30 seconds. Test the cakes by inserting a skewer into the centre – if it comes out clean, they're ready. If not, return to the microwave for 15 seconds and test again.
5. Leave the cakes to cool for 5 minutes before serving, dusted heavily with icing sugar.

MAKES: **2** | PREP TIME: **15 MINS** | COOKING TIME: **1 MIN 30 SECS**

Chocolate and Star Anise Mug Cakes

55 g / 2 oz / ¼ cup butter, softened
55 g / 2 oz / ¼ cup caster (superfine) sugar
1 large egg
55 g / 2 oz / ⅓ cup self-raising flour, sifted
2 tbsp unsweetened cocoa powder
½ tsp ground star anise, plus extra for sprinkling
2 tbsp dark hot chocolate sauce

1. Beat the butter and sugar together in a mug until pale and smooth.
2. Break the egg into a second mug and add the vanilla extract. Beat gently with a fork, then gradually stir the egg into the butter mixture.
3. Fold in the flour, cocoa and star anise, then spoon half of the mixture into the mug you used to beat the egg and level the tops.
4. Transfer the mugs to a microwave and cook on full power for 1 minute 30 seconds or until well risen and springy.
5. Leave the cakes to cool for 5 minutes, then top with chocolate sauce and add an extra sprinkle of ground star anise.

MAKES: **2** | PREP TIME: **20 MINS** | COOKING TIME: **2 MINS**

Chocolate Lava Mug Cakes

55 g / 2 oz / ¼ cup butter, softened
55 g / 2 oz / ¼ cup caster (superfine) sugar
1 large egg
55 g / 2 oz / ⅓ cup self-raising flour, sifted
2 tbsp unsweetened cocoa powder, plus extra for sprinkling
4 chocolate truffles
2 tbsp whipped cream
2 tbsp dark hot chocolate sauce
4 raspberries

1. Beat the butter and sugar together in a mug until pale and smooth.
2. Break the egg into a second mug and beat gently with a fork, then gradually stir the egg into the butter mixture.
3. Fold in the flour and cocoa powder, then spoon half of the mixture into the mug you used to beat the egg and level the tops. Push the truffles into the centre of each cake, then spoon 1 tablespoon of water on top of each one.
4. Transfer the mugs to a microwave and cook on full power for 2 minutes.
5. Leave to cool for 5 minutes, then pipe a rosette of cream on top of each one. Drizzle with chocolate sauce and garnish with raspberries, then serve immediately.

MAKES: 2 | PREP TIME: 15 MINS | COOKING TIME: 1 MIN 30 SECS

Rich Chocolate Chip Mug Cakes

55 g / 2 oz / ¼ cup butter, softened

55 g / 2 oz / ¼ cup caster (superfine) sugar

1 large egg

55 g / 2 oz / ⅓ cup self-raising flour, sifted

1 tbsp cocoa powder

3 tbsp milk chocolate chunks

2 tbsp milk chocolate, melted

1 handful of white and dark chocolate chips

1. Beat the butter and sugar together in a mug until pale and smooth.

2. Break the egg into a second mug and beat gently with a fork, then gradually stir the egg into the butter mixture.

3. Fold in the flour and cocoa powder, followed by the chocolate chunks, and then spoon half of the mixture into the mug you used to beat the egg and level the tops.

4. Transfer the mugs to a microwave and cook on full power for 1 ½ minutes. Test the cakes by inserting a skewer into the centre – if it comes out clean, the cakes are ready. If not, return to the microwave for 15 seconds and test again.

5. Leave the cakes to stand for 5 minutes, then pour 1 tablespoon of melted chocolate over each one.

6. Sprinkle each mug cake with the chocolate chips and serve immediately.

Toppings

MAKES: **200 ML** | PREP TIME: **5 MINS** | COOKING TIME: **5 MINS**

Dark Hot Chocolate Sauce

100 ml / 3 ½ fl. oz / ½ cup double (heavy) cream
1 tbsp runny honey
1 tbsp brandy
100 g / 3 ½ oz / ⅔ cup dark chocolate (minimum 70% cocoa solids), chopped

1. Put the cream, honey and brandy in a small saucepan and heat to simmering point.
2. Put the chopped chocolate in a heatproof bowl and pour over the cream.
3. Wait for 30 seconds, then stir gently until emulsified.
4. Immediately spoon over your mug cakes.

MAKES: 200 ML | PREP TIME: 5 MINS

Classic Buttercream

100 g / 3 ½ oz / ½ cup butter, softened
200 g / 7 oz / 2 cups icing (confectioner's) sugar
1 tsp vanilla extract

1. Beat the butter until smooth with an electric whisk.
2. Gradually incorporate the icing sugar, whisking all the time, until smooth.
3. Whisk in the vanilla extract and add a few drops of hot water if necessary to reach your desired consistency.
4. Spoon or pipe on top of your mug cakes.

Mixed Berry Jam

450 g / 1 lb / 2 cups granulated sugar

450 g / 1 lb / 3 cups raspberries,
strawberries and blueberries

1 lemon, juiced

1. Preheat the oven to 110°C (90° fan) / 225F / gas ¼.
2. Put the sugar in a heatproof bowl and transfer it to the oven along with two glass jars while you start cooking the fruit.
3. Put the berries and lemon juice in a large saucepan and cover with a lid. Heat gently for 10 minutes or until they soften in the juice they produce.
4. Stir in the warmed sugar until it dissolves, then increase the heat and boil until the mixture reads 107°C (225F) on a sugar thermometer.
5. Leave the jam to cool and thicken for 10 minutes then ladle into the prepared jars and seal with clean lids or waxed paper.
6. Spoon on top of your mug cakes for extra fruity flavour.

Cocoa Ripple Meringues

100 g / 3 ½ oz / ½ cup caster
(superfine) sugar

4 large egg whites

¼ tsp cream of tartar

2 tbsp unsweetened cocoa powder

1. Preheat the oven to 200°C (180°C fan) / 400F / gas 6 and line a large baking tray with greaseproof paper.
2. Spread the sugar out on the baking tray and heat in the oven for 8 minutes. Meanwhile, whisk the egg whites and cream of tartar in a freestanding mixer until stiff.
3. When the sugar is ready, remove it from the oven and reduce the temperature to 140°C (120°C fan) / 275F / gas 1. Pour the hot sugar in a slow continuous stream into the egg whites, whisking all the time. Continue to whisk on high speed for 10 minutes or until the side of the bowl feels cold.
4. Sieve the cocoa powder over the top, then fold and ripple it through with a large metal spoon. Space out heaped spoonfuls of the meringue on the baking tray.
5. Transfer the tray to the oven and bake for 1 hour. Turn off the oven and leave the meringues to cool slowly inside before serving.
6. Delicious crumbled over the top of mug cakes.

MAKES: **450 G** | PREP TIME: **5 MINS** | COOKING: **3 HOURS** | COOLING: **2 HOURS**

Nutty Dulce de Leche

1 x 400 g / 14 oz can sweetened condensed milk, unopened
50 g / 1 ¾ oz / ½ cup hazelnuts, chopped
25 g / 1 oz / ¼ cup almonds, chopped

1. Put the unopened can of condensed milk in a saucepan of water and simmer for 3 hours. Check the water level occasionally to ensure it doesn't boil dry.
2. Leave the can to cool completely before opening.
3. Spoon the dulce de leche into a bowl and beat until smooth. Fold in two thirds of the nuts, then sprinkle the rest on top.
4. Spoon on top of your mug cakes for extra flavour.

MAKES: **250 ML** | PREP TIME: **5 MINS**

Mint Chocolate Buttercream

100 g / 3 ½ oz / ½ cup butter, softened

200 g / 7 oz / 2 cups icing (confectioner's) sugar

2 tbsp unsweetened cocoa powder

1 tbsp whole milk

a few drops peppermint extract

1. Beat the butter until smooth with an electric whisk.

2. Gradually incorporate the icing sugar, whisking all the time, until smooth.

3. Stir the cocoa powder, milk and peppermint extract together, then whisk the mixture into the buttercream.

4. Spoon or pipe the buttercream on top of your mug cakes for extra indulgence and flavour.

Vanilla Custard

450 ml / 12 ½ fl. oz / 1 ¾ cups whole milk
1 vanilla pod, split lengthways
4 large egg yolks
75 g / 2 ½ oz / ⅓ cup caster
    (superfine) sugar

1. Combine the milk and vanilla pod in a saucepan and bring to simmering point, then turn off the heat and leave to infuse for 20 minutes.
2. Whisk the egg yolks with the caster sugar until thick.
3. Gradually incorporate the hot milk, whisking all the time, then scrape the mixture back into the saucepan.
4. Stir the custard over a low heat until it just starts to thicken, then put the base of the pan in cold water and continue to stir until the custard cools a little and the danger of curdling has passed.
5. Serve warm.

Fudge

300 ml / 10 ½ fl. oz / 1 ¼ cups whole milk
100 g / 3 ½ oz / ½ cup butter
350 g / 12 oz / 1 ½ cups caster
    (superfine) sugar

1. Oil an 18 cm (7 in) square cake tin. Put the milk, butter and caster sugar in a large, heavy-based saucepan and stir over a low heat to dissolve the sugar. Increase the temperature a little and bring to the boil.
2. Boil the mixture for 35 minutes or until it reaches 115°C (240F) on a sugar thermometer, stirring constantly.
3. Remove the pan from the heat and continue to stir for 5 minutes.
4. Scrape the mixture into the prepared tin and level the surface with a palate knife. Leave to cool completely.
5. Turn the fudge out of the tin in one piece and cut into squares with a sharp knife.
6. Delicious grated on top of a mug cake or cut into small pieces and stirred into your cake mixture before baking.

Salted Caramel Spread

100 g / 3 ½ oz / ½ cup butter
100 g / 3 ½ oz / ½ cup muscovado sugar
100 g / 3 ½ oz / ⅓ cup golden syrup
50 ml / 1 ¾ fl. oz / ¼ cup double
(heavy) cream
½ tsp sea salt

1. Put all of the ingredients in a small saucepan and stir over a low heat until the sugar dissolves.
2. Increase the heat to medium and simmer for 4 minutes, stirring occasionally.
3. Pour the sauce into a sterilised jar and leave to cool.
4. Store the caramel spread in the fridge before using.
5. Swirl into your mug cake mixture before cooking for added flavour or spoon on top of a cooked mug cake for decoration.

Crunchy Chocolate Chip Cookies

225 g / 8 oz / 1 ½ cups plain
(all-purpose) flour
75 g / 2 ½ oz / ⅓ cup caster
(superfine) sugar
150 g / 5 oz / ⅔ cup butter, cubed
50 g / 1 ¾ oz / ¼ cup chocolate chips

1. Preheat the oven to 180°C (160°C fan) / 350F / gas 4 and line a baking tray with greaseproof paper.
2. Mix together the flour and caster sugar in a bowl, then rub in the butter. Knead gently with the chocolate chips until the mixture forms a smooth dough then divide it into 16 pieces.
3. Roll each piece of dough into a ball, then press it onto the baking tray.
4. Bake the cookies for 18 minutes, turning the tray round halfway through. Transfer the cookies to a wire rack and leave to cool.
5. Delicious crumbled up on top of your mug cakes or mixed into the mug cake mixture before cooking for added crunch.

MAKES: **600 G** | PREP TIME: **15 MINS** | COOKING TIME: **5 MINS**

Chocolate Hazelnut Spread

200 ml / 7 fl. oz / ¾ cup double cream
150 g / 5 ½ oz / 1 cup dark chocolate, minimum 70% cocoa solids, chopped
150 g / 5 ½ oz / 1 cup milk chocolate, chopped
200 g / 7 oz / 1 ⅔ cups roasted hazelnuts, skinned
2 tbsp hazelnut oil (or sunflower if unavailable)
2 tbsp icing (confectioner's) sugar

1. Heat the cream until it starts to simmer, then pour it over the chopped chocolate and leave to stand for 30 seconds. Stir gently together until just combined.
2. Put the hazelnuts in a liquidizer with the oil and icing sugar. Grind to an oily paste, pausing to scrape down the sides occasionally.
3. Scrape the chocolate mixture into the liquidizer and blend again until very smooth.
4. Scrape into a bowl or jar and leave to cool completely before serving spooned on top of your mug cakes.

MAKES: 400 ML | PREP TIME: 15 MINS | COOKING TIME: 8 MINS

Cinnamon Caramel Sauce

100 ml / 3 ½ fl. oz / ½ cup double (heavy) cream
100 g / 3 ½ oz / ½ cup butter
100 g / 3 ½ oz / ⅓ cup golden syrup
100 g / 3 ½ oz / ½ cup muscovado sugar
1 tsp ground cinnamon

1. Put all of the ingredients in a small saucepan and stir over a low heat until the sugar dissolves.
2. Increase the heat to medium and simmer for 2 minutes, stirring occasionally.
3. Leave the sauce to cool for 10 minutes before serving warm, spooned over your mug cakes.

MAKES: **25** | PREP TIME: **45 MINS** | COOKING: **10 MINS** | SETTING: **2 HOURS**

Strawberry and Vanilla Marshmallows

2 tbsp cornflour (cornstarch)

8 gelatine leaves

250 g / 9 oz / 1 ¼ cups caster (superfine) sugar

1 vanilla pod, seeds only

50 ml / 1 ¾ fl. oz / ¼ cup strawberry syrup

1 large egg white

25 g / 1 oz / ¼ cup icing (confectioner's) sugar

1. Oil an 18 cm (7 in) square cake tin and dust it with cornflour. Put the gelatine leaves in a shallow bowl and cover them with 50 ml of cold water.

2. Put the caster sugar in a small saucepan with 135 ml of cold water then stir over a low heat until the sugar has dissolved. Increase the heat and let the mixture boil without stirring until it reaches 120°C (248F) on a sugar thermometer. Take the pan off the heat and carefully stir in the gelatine with its soaking water, the vanilla seeds and strawberry syrup.

3. Whisk the egg whites in a freestanding mixer until they form stiff peaks, then pour in the gelatine syrup in a thin stream with the whisk still running. Continue to whisk for 10 minutes on high speed while the marshmallow cools.

4. Scrape the mixture into the tin and level the top, then leave to set for 2 hours. Turn the marshmallow out of the tin onto a work surface that has been dusted with icing sugar. Dip a sharp knife into hot water, then cut the marshmallow into cubes, cleaning and re-dipping the knife as necessary.

MAKES: 24 | PREP TIME: 20 MINS | COOKING TIME: 1 HOUR

Mini Meringues

4 large egg whites

100 g / 3 ½ oz / ½ cup caster (superfine) sugar

1. Preheat the oven to 140°C (120°C fan) / 275F / gas 1 and oil and line a large baking tray with greaseproof paper.
2. Whisk the egg whites with an electric whisk until stiff, then gradually whisk in half the caster sugar until the mixture is very shiny. Fold in the remaining caster sugar with a large metal spoon, being careful to retain as much air as possible.
3. Spoon the meringue into a piping bag fitted with a large star nozzle and pipe small rosettes onto the baking tray.
4. Transfer the tray to the oven and bake for 1 hour. Turn off the oven and leave the meringues to cool slowly inside before serving on top of your mug cakes.
5. Alternatively, crumble the meringue over your mug cakes for added texture.

SERVES: 4 | PREP TIME: 5 MINS | COOKING TIME: 10 MINS

Zabaglione

3 large egg yolks
2 ½ tbsp caster (superfine) sugar
2 ½ tbsp Marsala

1. Set a heatproof bowl over a saucepan of simmering water, making sure the bottom of the bowl does not come into contact with the water.
2. Add the egg yolks, sugar and Marsala to the bowl and whisk vigorously until the mixture thickens.
3. The zabaglione is ready when you can drizzle a line of the mixture off the whisk back into the bowl and the trail stays visible for a few seconds.
4. Remove the bowl from the saucepan and serve immediately.

Index